upside
umop
FREEDOM

upside
down
FREEDOM

INVERTED PRINCIPLES FOR CHRISTIAN LIVING

taylor field

NEW HOPE
PUBLISHERS
Gospel-Centered. Missions-Driven.

BIRMINGHAM, ALABAMA

New Hope® Publishers
P. O. Box 12065
Birmingham, AL 35202-2065
NewHopeDigital.com
New Hope Publishers is a division of WMU®.

Library of Congress Cataloging-in-Publication Data
Field, Taylor.
  Upside-down freedom : inverted principles for Christian living / Taylor Field.
    pages cm
  ISBN 978-1-59669-376-0 (pbk.)
  1. Christian life. 2. Liberty--Religious aspects--Christianity. I. Title.
  BV4501.3.F533 2013
  248.4--dc23
                         2012051768

ISBN-10: 1-59669-376-2
ISBN-13: 978-1-59669-376-0

N134117 • 0613 • 2M1

Dedicated to

the courageous people in the Lower East Side who, through 26 years of "recovery" groups, asked the hard questions about biblical freedom.

> Approach
> The inverse image of my home
> From a puddle on the street
> The dark umbrella at the steps
> Its bright top pointed to my feet—
> I'm only free to see my door
> Then walk all dry in rain about
> When I turn puddles right side up
> Under something inside out.
>
> TAYLOR FIELD

> "Stone walls do not a prison make."
> *Richard Lovelace, 24-year-old, long-haired poet in the seventeenth century*

Acknowledgments

—To Susan, my wife, and to my sons and daughters-in-law, Freeman, Candace, Owen, and Krista, who all remind me that right side up may be upside down.

—To the workers at New Hope Publishers, especially Andrea Mullins and Joyce Dinkins, for being willing to look at familiar things and find the unfamiliar.

—To my co-workers at Graffiti, who help me learn to laugh when I don't really want to.

*T*able of *C*ontents

introduction
The Cage Within
a Cage

"Whoever seeks to preserve his life will lose it, but whoever loses his life will keep it."

JESUS, LUKE 17:33

"There is always an easy solution to every human problem — neat, plausible, and wrong."

—H. L. Mencken

Doing the Opposite

On August 5, 1949, 16 people were fighting a fire in the Mann Gulch area of Montana. Fifteen of the men were "smokejumpers," highly skilled workers who parachuted out of airplanes to get to a fire. It was a very hot day, with turbulent wind. At one point, the conditions on the slope, with the combination of heat and the fast burning high grass, caused a "blow up." With this extreme increase of fire line intensity, the deadly fire was now moving dangerously fast toward the firefighters. To escape, the men would have to run up a ridge.

As the conditions became more imminent, the foreman of the crew, Wagner Dodge, ordered the men to drop their heavy tools so they could run more easily. Soon Dodge realized that they would not make the ridge line in front of the fire. At this point, he did what was to many people a remarkable thing. In this kind of extreme fiery roar and heat, I imagine that everything in you would tell you to run up the ridge to escape to freedom. Instead, in the middle of that impending danger and noise, Dodge stopped, took out some matches, bent down, and started a fire, burning an area of grass before the main fire got to him. In doing so, he was attempting to create an "escape fire," a burned-out area where he could lie down as the larger fire went past.

This action was not part of any of the smokejumpers' training. The rest of the workers thought he was crazy. Later, Dodge just said that it simply seemed the logical thing to do. As the fire rushed toward them, Dodge tried to direct the men to come up to the burned-out area. "This way," he kept calling to the crew behind in the midst of the smoke and the roar. "This way!" It is not clear whether the other smokejumpers, skilled young men, understood his directions. They had another answer. Dodge stated that he heard one of them say, "To hell with that, I'm getting out of here."

Fifteen of the men made a run for it up the ridge to escape the fire. Thirteen of them died. All of this happened very quickly. At 5:45 P.M. the men realized their danger. By 5:56 P.M., the intense blaze had swept over them. We know the exact time because the heat of the fire melted the hands in place on a smokejumper's wristwatch as the fire passed.

The tragedy spawned many reforms and reflections. One of the reforms was further training for these talented, independent, young men who were drawn to be smokejumpers. Their training was more balanced in helping them to think quickly, but also to follow the commands of their foreman in times of danger, even when those instructions did not make immediate sense.

Sometimes life is like that. We think we know how to get to freedom. Instead, we have to do the opposite. That's what this book is about.

The Genius of Pleasure Island

The perception of doing the opposite of what we expect is deep in the human psyche. In a way, part of human freedom means returning to the obvious. We all know that what sometimes seems to be freedom is not. We often watch on TV the people who seem to have all the equipment for amazing freedom. They have astonishing wealth and are heirs to fortunes. Then we hear that they overdose on drugs in their lonely mansions. We see people with great beauty and talent, with all the right connections in the entertainment world, going to rehab for the fourth time. We see writers with great intelligence and fame, unbelievable recognition and prestige, found dead in apparent suicides. How can this be? They have all the accoutrements of a wide scope of options, don't they? Wealth, fame, beauty, adoration, recognition, charm, good looks, intellect, wit, and yet, they seem so sad, so trapped. It is one of the paradoxes of freedom. The people who sometimes seem as though they should be the freest, turn out to be in some kind of bondage.

The Bible uses an image that we have become somewhat unfamiliar with. It is the image of a snare. A snare is a trap for a bird or another animal. I suppose we can still think of an old-time mousetrap, with its attractive cheese used as bait. The snare looks as though it might provide something good, such as food, but in the end, it is designed to be a bondage. It is amazing how often the Bible uses this image. And the story is told over and over in almost every society. The truth of the story is sometimes forgotten because the way it is expressed sounds corny, so much like a cliché.

I remember watching the animated movie *Pinocchio* as a child. It was already an old movie when I saw it for the first time.

Pinocchio is a person made of wood, who wants to become a real boy. Yet he has trouble doing so. At one point he is lured up to a place called, not too subtly, Pleasure Island. It all sounds good, so natural. Rides and candy and cigars and pool. But it is a snare. In order to be really free, Pinocchio would have to do the opposite of what he felt like doing. By being on the island, and acting like jackasses, the boys turn into donkeys and are eventually sold to the circus or used as beasts of burden.

I remember as a child looking at Pinocchio's donkey ears. He had already started to change. By going after what he thought was freedom, ironically, he began to become more subhuman. It happens all the time.

How to Train an Elephant

I have spent much of my life working with people with clearly destructive addictions, in Hong Kong, San Francisco, and New York City. This is what I have learned — that often no matter how much the bondage feels as though it comes from outside circumstances, it doesn't. In the end, bondage isn't really made up of the roar of a fire or the pay off at some pleasure island.

All of us know that it is really an inside job, but each of us thinks it only applies to other people, not to us. The Internet is full of stories about how they train elephants in India. A large six-ton elephant will only be tied by a thin rope, but it will not break free. As a young elephant, it had a strong chain on its leg, and learned that it could not break free. As it grew older, the bonds were lessened because the bonds were unnecessary. The bonds were now in the elephant's mind.

I have never trained an elephant, but where I grew up, we had barbed wire fences for cattle. Sometimes, when it was tough to set up a barbed wire fence, we would run an electric line. If a cow touched the electric line, it would get a shock, and then the cow would avoid it. If we had to turn the electricity off to repair something in the system, I saw that the cows still avoided it. The enclosure was no longer in the cows' circumstances; the enclosure was now in the cows' minds. During the repair, the cows could have easily broken through the enclosure in a minute. But they didn't.

I call this a cage within a cage. The outside cage is represented by the fence. These are the outside circumstances. But the inside cage is in the mind.

Somehow we have been twisted in our training to think that following God is about confinement, as if God were some kind of cramping force. Eugene Peterson, the translator of *The Message*, reminds us of the core message: "The root meaning in Hebrew of 'salvation' is to be broad, to become spacious, to enlarge. It carries the sense of deliverance from an existence that has become compressed, confined, and cramped" [God's Message for Each Day, page 161]. We can't get around it. God is a freedom fighter.

One of the most important narratives in the entire Bible is about freedom. In the story, the people of God are slaves. It seems as though they have been slaves for centuries. In an undeniably miraculous way, God delivers them from bondage, from Egypt, and from the Pharaoh's selfish and oppressive ways. They go through the desert, the place of their ancestors long ago. They complain at almost every step. They learn how to depend on God for everything, for direction, for water, for food. Slaves who may not have touched a weapon for generations have to learn how to fight.

Finally, they make it to the border of the Promised Land. This is the moment they have been waiting for and praying for—a place to be where they are not slaves. They send out people to give a report, and they learn that there are giants in the land. Their own people feel like grasshoppers.

Here is Pharaoh's greatest trick and revenge. The people have escaped. They are long gone. The Pharaoh who enslaved them is dead. The past of working and being beaten is over. Yet Pharaoh and Egypt are still within their minds. After dwelling in complaint and blame, the people continue:

"And they said to one another, 'Let us choose a leader and go back to Egypt'" (Numbers 14:4).

Are they crazy? Have they convinced themselves of an idealized past that never was? Are they merely going to go back to familiar patterns, because what lies ahead is something different and challenging? This scene represents the cage within a cage. The people are on the border of the Promised Land, and they have already been delivered, and they are talking themselves into returning to a life of bondage. Somehow, Pharaoh is still inside their heads, and somehow, he still controls them. As the old saying goes, it took one day for the people of God to get out of Egypt. It took 40 years for Egypt to get out of the people of God. People in Alcoholics Anonymous (AA) describe this mode of reasoning, planning, and justifying a return to bondage, as stinking thinking. Well, it certainly does stink.

Mind Cages

This kind of thinking is so real to me because I see it so often. Let me share what happened to me recently with a man I will call Jack. I have known of Jack for many years in the park here in the Lower East Side. He considers himself a free spirit, partying, demonstrating, drinking, drugging, doing what he likes when he likes. He prided himself in being a free spirit, and he isn't too interested in me.

One day he came to one of our meals at our church, and he asked to use my cell phone. I said sure, and we made a phone call. Once he was on the phone, his tone changed completely. "Ma," he pleaded, "it's Jack. Please, Ma, don't hang up, Ma. Things are different this time, Ma. I'm not drinking anymore, Ma, really."

I might add at this point that Jack reeked of alcohol and I could see the bottle hanging out of his coat pocket.

"Ma," he continued. "Ma, I'm with a *pastor*."

Jack turned to me and put the phone in my hand. "Go ahead, tell her, tell her I'm not drinking."

I could hear the hopeful tremor in the poor woman's voice. I could not tell her what Jack wanted me to say.

Jack took the phone back and continued to beg and cry. "Let me come home, Ma, please let me come home. Things will be different this time, Ma."

Eventually, Jack gave me back the phone, and he left. A few weeks later, he marched up to me at the end of a Sunday morning service. He had never come to a church service before, and he had just slipped in at the end. "I want to use your cell phone to call my mother," he demanded, heedless of the people around him.

I simply said no. I wasn't going to be a part of his deceit. He was shocked. I said something I have said a number of times. "We can't help you anymore, Jack, unless you allow us to become a part of your life." He couldn't believe it. He stomped off through the crowd.

In the following weeks, every time I passed him in the park, he cursed me with a sneer. He called me a traitor. He showed his contempt for someone like me who pretended to be a Christian.

I don't care. I'm not going away. And Jack's story isn't over yet. But think of the irony of Jack's situation. He thinks he is free, being able to do what he wants. He considers himself young, but now he is really a middle aged man. Still, he is not beneath calling his mother and lying as the weather gets colder and it gets more unpleasant to stay out all night every night. He is not even aware that a pastor might not help him lie. Even sadder, he has convinced himself in his mind that the situation is my fault, that he is the victim. His way of thinking has gone on so long, that he doesn't even realize what has happened. Jack has a horrible cage within his mind, and he thinks he is a free spirit, subject to none.

I don't mean to give Jack a hard time. I have mind cages, too—scripts inside my head that keep me bound, and I don't even realize it.

Deuteronomy 28 gives a wonderful set of results if we listen to the voice of God (v. 1). One of the results is this: *"And the Lord will make you the head and not the tail"* (v. 13). One of the things we continue to learn on the streets is that the first step in ceasing to be the victim of circumstances is to stop thinking like a tail. It is the constant thinking like a tail that is the cage within the cage.

Without a doubt, circumstances can make us feel bound or imprisoned. We can be bound by real walls, or lack of finances, or lack of opportunities, or a physical ailment. We can feel trapped in a job and responsibilities that look as though they have no exit. But there is a way of living that refuses to let the circumstances define us. There is a way to move from the overwhelming bondage of circumstances to a freedom from circumstances. I have seen it happen, over and over.

Freedom turns out to be a puzzle within a puzzle. People in recovery will often go to the story that Jesus told of the son who wants his money now while he is still young and can enjoy it. It sounds good for a while. Surely this is the way to true freedom. But his approach turns out to be stinking thinking. Eventually he finds himself in a pig pen, realizing that he is acting worse than a servant from his former life. Not free at all, anymore.

"My transgressions were bound into a yoke," Jeremiah says (Lamentations 1:14). The worst is when the bondage becomes the script of life and gets branded inside your head. We don't even realize what is happening. In our recovery groups, we are often reminded that the word for Satan in Hebrew means "the accuser." Perhaps the accuser's best weapon is when *"the dog returns to its own vomit"* (2 Peter 2:22). No chains or leashes are involved, no outside force. Then the guilt comes.

Simple Answers Can Be Treasonous

In thinking about freedom, the quick answer may not be the truest. Recently, I read a book by a rabbi named Abraham Joshua Heschel. He was arrested by the Gestapo in Poland during World War II. His sister was killed in a German bombing. His mother was murdered by the Nazis, and his other two sisters died in Nazi concentration camps. He wrote a deep book, reflecting on the struggles and agonies the major and minor prophets in the Bible went through. Often answers in the prophetic writings don't come easily or quickly. You could tell that as he talked about the agonies some of the prophets went through in sharing God's Word in their time, he was reflecting on God's work in his own time. He made this comment that hit me like a hammer: "In theology, shallowness is treason."

Sometimes we are so confident we know what freedom is when we talk about politics or patriotism. But freedom has its own twists and turns, and a shallow treatment can become its own bondage. Freedom doesn't always respond to the easiest answer. If freedom means being able to think and act without compulsion, not being restricted or confined, then we must think deeply. The complexities and turns of the experiences of life will force us to think again about freedom in a lot of different ways.

Strangely enough, bondage is sometimes the path to freedom. We see the sad ironies of freedom. Some people see great freedom in the way Francis of Assisi could embrace lepers and help the most wretched.

According to some stories, Francis of Assisi had to spend time in a cave, sick and defeated, after having the wealth and privilege of an honored soldier. Only then does he begin to get a hint of another way to freedom, a freedom that changed his society.

People sense intuitively that the journey to freedom is often inverted. Albert Herbert, the British religious artist, has painted a wonderful picture of Jonah. In the picture, we can see Jonah inside a great seagoing creature. Jonah, however, is naked and looks almost like an infant. The artist has made Jonah look as though he is just ready for a new birth. The painting raises questions. Was Jonah free when he was determining his own fate, running as fast as he could from Nineveh? Or did Jonah become free when he was far away from any support, deep in the ocean, enclosed by a fish, uttering praises to God in the dark? It seems paradoxical.

The older I get, the more I see that paradox seems to be a part of most things important. Niels Bohr, the Danish physicist, spent a lot of time discussing what he had found as at the subatomic level as a scientist. He once said that, "You can recognize a small truth because its opposite is a falsehood. The opposite of a great truth is another truth."

In a previous book, *Upside-Down Leadership*, I talk about the importance of paradox in the Reformation and the renewed delight in going back to the Bible. Many of the truths that German theologian Martin Luther saw in the Bible are paradoxes. The paradoxes are two opposing truths put side by side, and if we only speak of one truth, we miss the point. We are sinner and we are saint, we are lord over all and servant to all, God is always hidden and always revealed. Luther could not get over the fact that as we talk about the omniscience of God, Paul also talks about the foolishness and weakness of God (1 Corinthians 1:25). To me, getting free is one of those paradoxes. In one sense, being free means not having any binding circumstances and having as many options to choose from as possible. Yet, on the other hand, we find in real life that sometimes we become most free in the midst of the most binding circumstances.

One of the servant deacons in our church was arrested eight times for being involved in Christian activities in Romania when it was a Communist state. The authorities would call him up from his cell at midnight and beat him in the face and pull his hair. He found himself in situations where everything was taken away from him.

He has had a hard life since he was set free. Sometimes I look at him at church and puzzle over the fact that he has a serenity in the midst of trouble that some of the younger people in the church, who have had unparalleled freedom in comparison, do not show. Why?

God the Freedom Fighter

*F*reedom is a continuing riddle for us as humans. One thing I know from reading the Bible is that God wants us to be free. He is the ultimate freedom fighter. He wants us truly to be free. The Bible speaks about freedom a lot. "Everyone who commits sin is a slave of sin," Jesus says. Then Jesus takes us to a place where we can think about freedom in a deeper way. *"So if the Son sets you free, you are free indeed,"* He says (John 8:34, 36).

We think of freedom as the sense of release from bondage of any kind. It is the refusal to be determined by oppressive forces. There seems to be more than one way to be free. One way to be free is to have everything. With enough wealth, external power, or fame, one may feel that he or she has an infinite number of choices to make. In this route, there is a certain kind of freedom.

The other way to freedom is when we are developed on the inside to handle anything. Essentially it is an inside job. I have the privilege of working with one of my heroes in freedom. Every time he encounters something difficult, he says, "I am going to the gym. This experience is making me stronger." Eventually, it is as James the brother of Jesus says, "Count it all joy . . . when you meet trials of various kinds" (James 1:2). Huh? That sounds insane. "For you know that the testing of your faith produces steadfastness, and let steadfastness have its full effect." I can understand that such an approach is like going to the gym. But the next line gives the result. *"That you may be perfect and complete, lacking in nothing"* (James 1:2–4). Lacking in nothing. That is freedom. But it is something that happens on the inside, not something that is dependent on circumstances. It is an inside job.

Recently I went to Sequoia National Park. As a hard-core tree hugger, I was ecstatic. I love to spend time with oaks on the East Coast, oaks that may be 100 years old, or 200, or even 300 years old. I like to think that these trees were alive before my grandfather was born, and they may continue to be alive when my grandchildren have passed away. Yet in a grove of sequoias, I was walking among trees that were 1,000 years old, or 2,000 years old, or even 3,000 years old. How did they do it? As I read about these noble trees, I saw that they had the ability to encounter hardship without dying. They were able to heal, even if there was fire, or flood, or lightning. The floods and the fires came. But they had an ability, so to speak, on the inside, to handle them. That is freedom.

In Isaiah 61, the Servant speaks about raising up a new kind of people. These were the people that were mourning and in ashes. The Servant is to make them so that they are called "the oaks of righteousness, the planting of the Lord" (v. 3). This is the kind of freedom we want, not the freedom to avoid hardships, but to survive them.

Sad to say it, but a lot of the Bible was written by murderers. I wish it weren't so, and I venture to say that at some level, God wishes it weren't so also. Moses killed a man in Egypt and fled because of it. Yet he is responsible for the first five books of the Bible. David killed a man for the sake of his own convenience, yet we sing the lyrics of his songs all the time. Paul consented to the murder of Christians, yet he wrote a lot of the New Testament. Each of these people had to deal with being fugitives, or being in prison, or being chased by authorities. Yet I believe each has something to say about freedom. We often talk about people who are in prison as people who are *incarcerated*. The word comes from the Latin words *in* and *carcer*, which are the English words for "in" and "prison." These three biblical characters had to deal with exile and caves and prisons, because of the authorities and circumstances of the times. Somehow, God taught them through these things about freedom. Even in confining circumstances, they learned to be unbound inside. I call them the "uncarcerated" (see the appendix). As we work through some opposite principles for freedom, these three people can help us.

We are going to look at ten upside-down ways to look at freedom. In the story at the beginning of this introduction, the foreman tried to show his fellow firefighters the way to be free from the flames. Instead of running from the enormous danger, the answer lay in pulling out a little book of matches, lighting the grass right around him, and lying down in the ashes. It was the opposite of what one thought was the right thing to do. The answer was a bit upside down.

In one sense, I don't have any right to write about these things. I have been blessed beyond measure my entire life. Yet for 35 years, I have been with people who were often in deep, outward bondage, people who were homeless, or strapped by poverty, or bound by a chemical addiction, or encased by experiences of child abuse. I have watched some go deeper and deeper into bondage, and I have watched some die because of the bondage. It is a real battle, and there have been real casualties. On the other hand, I have watched some, in spite of absolutely horrible circumstances, find amazing release through Christ and the Word of God. I long to see that kind of freedom for every person, and I think there are some practical ways to find that release. I think the same principles work for everyone, even for those whose bondage is much more hidden from public view.

I heard a TV preacher recently say that we want to be "the devil's worst nightmare." I like that phrase. I have watched people find release and walk out and help others in extreme bondage find release. That is my dream—that these people, who have been changed on the inside, despite overwhelmingly bad odds, walk into the urban areas of despair and heartache. I pray that they become "the devil's worst nightmare". I hope everyone who reads this book becomes the devil's worst nightmare too. It is our birthright to do so.

Every day, in our work in the Lower East Side in New York City, I feel as though I sit at the feet of giants of freedom. They may not always fit society's view of freedom or success. To me, these people are the truly uncarcerated. I have no right to speak for them, but I can tell you what I am learning from being with them. Their freedom shouts out in unexpected places.

Ronald Finally Says Something

I am learning that the cry for freedom cannot be categorized or limited to one form of answer. Even when the outer cage seems most oppressive, the doors can fly open on the inside. I remember something that happened just recently. It wasn't a bright day. The Monday morning couldn't have been drearier, and I felt as though I was going to the dreariest place in the world. I was accompanied by some students who were on a mission trip to New York City. They were up for anything, but they had no idea what they were getting into. We were going to an old nursing home where our church went every week. The home had just been told they had been bought up by a developer, and they were going to be closed down. The morale of the staff and the patients couldn't have been worse.

We gathered together in a pathetic group to hold a protestant worship service together. Seven patients lined up in a row—all in wheelchairs. Some could not even lift their heads. Ronald was one of the quiet ones there in his wheelchair. We had known him for a long time. He smiled kindly at all of us. Being a good Episcopalian, he was always respectful as we worshipped and sang the few hymns in the tattered song books.

The students sang some songs and read some Scriptures and gave some testimonies. They were cheery, even though you could hear people groaning and crying out down the halls in the background. The students didn't want to preach, so I did. We started off slow, in our little group of wheelchairs, but I guess I started getting caught up in my own eloquence. I suppose I forgot the absurdity of what I was saying in this oppressive environment. I had been preaching a series on freedom on Sunday morning, and so I talked about how the people of God had been slaves in Egypt for hundreds of years. For generations they had forgotten how to "stand tall" as God puts it in Leviticus. I told them how God delivered the people out of Egypt and then had them fight the tribes in the desert, perhaps as training. I told them about my co-worker, because every time he encountered a frustrating and irritating circumstance, he said, "This is good practice! This will make me stronger."

I don't know what I was saying to these poor people, trapped in their wheelchairs in the dingy, depressing environment. I could see Ronald's head, propped against the side of his chair, with his eyes closed as he listened.

My voice began to rise as I got excited. "You don't want to just vegetate, do you? You don't want your spiritual muscles to get flaccid, do you?" Remember the people listening were in wheelchairs. What was I saying? My voice got louder as I reached my final challenging question. "You don't want to be spiritual couch potatoes, do you?"

Quiet Ronald couldn't contain himself anymore. He had never spoken in worship before. Clearly he was with me, and shouted out words that came from the bottom of his heart.

"Hell no!" he bellowed with conviction.

Even I shut up for a moment. The eyes of the student mission team got as big as frying pans. I think they were expecting a milder experience at a nursing home. "Well, that's right, Ronald," I said. "We are not going to take it lying down. We aren't going to give up before we get to the Promised Land."

That's it. Ronald didn't say another word the whole time. He smiled a knowing smile at me as I left.

The fact that Ronald said anything was a shock. The expletive that pierced the dreary, smelly room was memorable. But the more I thought about it, the more I began to listen to the words behind the words.

If I think about the cry from Ronald's heart, I think that his words might have been better than a "Hallelujah," for that particular moment and that particular time. To me, he was saying with clear sincerity that he refused to let the wheelchair and his rapidly declining vigor be the things that defined him. He refused to let the fear of being relocated to some other urban institution determine who he was. To me, it was one of the healthiest cries I have heard for a long time. In his own way, he was refusing to allow his outer circumstances to become his inner prison. May we say a resounding no along with Ronald.

principle #1
Learn to Hate—The Prison of Being Unaware

"O you who love the Lord, hate evil!"

PSALM 97:10

"I hate quotations. Tell me what you know."

—Ralph Waldo Emerson

Sad, Tiny Feet

My grandfather was a medical missionary to China in the early part of the twentieth century. He kept a remarkable collection of medical pictures of the infirmities of the people he ministered to. I looked back at one recently that was particularly repulsive to me. It was the picture of a horribly deformed foot. It seemed impossible that a person could walk on such a foot. The toes were curled under and the bones bent to a tiny shape.

My mother grew up in China. I remember her telling me of the wealthy aristocratic women who had their feet bound as children. The bones would grow into a much tinier space than they should. The women, according to my mom, could hardly walk. Still, the small feet were a sign of the women's wealth, and perhaps in some strange way, their femininity. Perhaps they saw it as a sign of elegance.

I have no way of evaluating what was happening in the Chinese culture at the time. I know every culture adopts ways that can seem odd and oppressive to others.

Still, I hated those pictures that my grandfather showed me. Still more, I hated the attitude, an approach to life where the victims were not really aware of the binding and crippling that they were subjected to. They had convinced themselves that their inability to walk was a sign of status.

Many of us can think of situations that we disliked because they seemed so confining. I remember looking into the face of a gorilla sitting forlornly in a glass cage at a zoo on a hot July afternoon. I remember looking at an exhibit of exquisite Bonsai trees, and yet somehow yearning for the trees to grow big and strong instead of being bound and clipped into miniature versions. I remember taking a daylong process to visit a teenager at the prison at Rikers Island. In each case, something rose up in me like revulsion. But in the end, I grew to learn that it is not the actual circumstance of the binding or the glass cage or the prison bars. It is the attitude to life that allows such bondage. As I said in the introduction, the God of the Bible is such a freedom fighter.

Perhaps the greatest prison for anyone is to be in bondage and to be unaware. That would be the ultimate cage of the mind. Perhaps that is part of hell—being trapped and not even knowing it. I think C. S. Lewis tries to portray this idea in *The Great Divorce*. He paints a picture of hell as a dreary, dark urban area ("grey town") with a bus departing to heaven. There is plenty of room on the bus, even though people keep fighting each other for the best place in the line. Most people are so convinced that they are their own little god that they do not even want to go on the bus. The ones that do go never seem to realize that the grey town they live in is hell.

Jesus the Hater

*I*t may seem strange to say that we are to learn to hate in a book based on Christ's principles. But in a way, it is true. In order to really love something, we are going to have to hate something. If I am to love the Jewish people, I am going to have to hate what the Holocaust did to them. If I am going to truly love people who are homeless, I am going to have to hate the bondage of chemical addiction.

David in the Psalms understood this, and described oppressive activity as evil: *"O you who love the Lord, hate evil! He preserves the lives of his saints; he delivers them from the hand of the wicked"* (Psalm 97:10).

Even Jesus, who is the advocate of love, is described as someone who hates.

This is what the Bible says about the Messiah in Hebrews 1:8–9: *"But of the Son he says, 'Your throne, O God is forever and ever, the scepter of uprightness is the scepter of your kingdom. You have loved righteousness and hated wickedness.'"*

Later we will talk about making our decisions through the path of love. That is the way of freedom. But in my work, I have come to realize that we must be trained sometimes in learning what to hate. So often we take the route of bondage, and somehow slip into hating some person. The Bible describes this path as walking in darkness (1 John 2:11). It's like turning out the lights before we walk across a room. If we hate the person, we become like the poor bull in a bull fight, rushing after the red cape when the real enemy is sinking darts into our shoulders.

No, we have been commanded as followers of Jesus to battle something, but it is to battle principalities and powers, not people (Ephesians 6:12). It is not flesh and blood we are to fight. Nor are we to hate flesh and blood. In fact, doing so will only bring further confusion and darkness.

But there is something we are to hate, because of the shrapnel and wounds and damage it causes. The Psalms sometimes speak of hating. We can chart a checkered path of hating in the lyrics of the songs there.

David was one of the songwriters. He had quite a journey with enemies. In the end, he was one who learned to act like a king regardless of his circumstances. After he was anointed as a king by Samuel, he found himself in a variety of situations. Sometimes he was in the palace, but he also found himself as a fugitive on the run. He found that he had no place to go and had to act as if he were mentally insane in order to survive. He lived in a cave. Many people tried to kill him. Even so, he learned to act like a king.

In the lyrics of his songs, he encourages those who love God to hate evil. I counted 31 times where the Book of Psalms uses the word *hate*. I counted 36 times in which the same book uses the word *love*.

As we read more deeply, we see the whole drama of the Bible from Genesis to Revelation. We see that God hates evil because it is so hurtful to us. It puts us in bondage. Sometimes the words of the prophets sound like shock therapy. Some things that seem only like mild misdemeanors in society to us—idolatry, systems that forget the poor, immorality—are disastrous from God's view. Sometimes this emphasis makes the whole Bible seem out of sync, or overdramatic, even odd.

Once we understand that the worst bondage is when we don't even know we are in bondage, then God's strong words make more sense.

How sad it would have been if Pinocchio had persisted doggedly at Pleasure Island, not being aware that he already had donkey ears, dogmatically insisting that Pleasure Island has helped him to be free. To be honest, I see this kind of thing all the time as I deal with people who are clearly chemically addicted. They proclaim their freedom to do anything they want, and they don't even realize the freedom they are pursuing is taking away their family, their relationships, their free choices, and ultimately, their lives.

I have watched some people work to score drugs while waiting in the emergency room of a hospital, their health horribly ruined because of their very use of those drugs. They don't see what is happening. Sometimes I feel that I am watching them become less human before my eyes, stealing from people who care for them, abusing those closest to them, living in a well of mirrors.

I am amazed at the kinds of reasons they promote to support their own bondage.

I understand their human attempt to justify; still, it saddens me. More than once, I have heard a person trapped in the hell of drinking or drugs tell me in explanation, "You see, my mother died two years ago," with a knowing look, thinking that this fact justifies the present state of human deterioration.

I have sometimes even said, "You think that your mother would be proud of what you are doing to yourself now? Do you think that this is the right way to honor your mom's passing? To me, this lack of awareness of the trap the person has been led to is the strongest sign of the most permanent bondage.

Recently, I spent time with a wonderful, charming man who daily proclaimed his freedom from the bonds of society, and at the same time, was constantly trying to figure a way to get enough money for the next drink. He was so well read and intelligent, with a delightful sense of humor. He still wrote sports articles even while living on the street. His aunt had been a famous actor. Ultimately, he fell while he was drinking and cracked his head. He died in the hospital alone. We only found out about it later. I truly hate what that bondage did to that wonderful man.

I don't mean to harp on people who are dealing with a chemical addiction. It is just one of the groups of people that I work with often in New York City. We all have our areas of vulnerability. We are all called to a new freedom in some sense. I see men and woman encaged by wealth, working themselves to death in the city, bringing themselves to a sterile, early grave, and they are not even aware of it. I see others who may not have much money, but base every single moral and vocational decision on financial factors. I see people who have all their outward needs met, but live in a cage of anxiety. I recently saw a friend at her own wedding, her face drawn with anxiety before the proceedings. I thought, *This is supposed to be a happy time. What happened for the experience to become such a burden of anxiety?*

I remember a woman many years ago who felt so guilty. She would stand outside our building but would not come in. She did not feel that she was worthy enough to come in. She was in a bondage that limited all that God had for her, and she thought she was being humble and religious. She was not aware of the prison she was in.

It may seem strange, but I have seen health come as people began to be aware of the bondage and began to hate that bondage. Alcoholics Anonymous sometimes calls it being sick and tired of being sick and tired. Yet it is the prison of oblivion, the prison of being unaware, that is the most dangerous. This experience can be even worse because we know that deep inside something is wrong, but somehow it would take too much for us to really see the truth. We don't even know what is happening, and we continue in misery, like the upper-class woman with bound feet, lording her superiority over a free-walking peasant.

A Constructive Hatred and a Constructive Anger

*I*t is a good exercise to think about what it is we hate. If it is a person, as 1 John points out, we have already turned out the lights and will find ourselves bumping against all the furniture. That kind of hatred doesn't allow us to see people as they really are. But there is a constructive kind of hatred, a hatred that hates the attitude of bondage. It breaks out of the prison of being unaware.

A constructive hatred can produce a constructive anger. Augustine is said to have stated that there are two beautiful daughters of hope—anger and courage. Anger at the way things are, and courage to see that they do not remain that way. We see an anger in Jesus when He looks at the silence of the religious people in Mark 3:5. We see an anger as Jesus sees the oppressive use religious people made of the temple with their systems of money in John 2:15. We can see how anger and courage can become the daughters of hope.

Many years ago, as I worked with a program in San Francisco that dealt with broken people who were often homeless, I found myself being tutored in emergency help by a stern woman who had worked with people in need for many years. "When I see a passive person, or a person who is docile, I don't see much hope for improvement. But when I see a person who is angry at their situation, I think it is a sign of health." This comment took me off guard, because even then I had seen a certain kind of blaming anger become a prison in itself (more about that later). But I have also seen that when that hatred of oppression rises up, the possibility of constructive action can also come.

Thomas Wolfe, the novelist from North Carolina, died at an early age. One of the last manuscripts he was working on before he died was a story about a boy who greatly admired his father (published in *The Hills Beyond*). His father was a kind and gentle man and served as a judge in the legal system in his small town. The boy watched his father's face redden and the veins of his forehead swell as he walked by a Civil War veteran who sat on the court stairs every day. The veteran had lost a leg in the Civil War, and thrived on the attention he got from other people hanging out on the stairs. He looked at people with imploring eyes to get people to help him stand with great drama. The judge was not impressed. The boy reminded his dad that the man had a wooden leg, after all. The father replied that a wooden leg is no excuse for anything. The boy didn't understand his father's harshness.

One day the boy was reading a book on the battles of the Civil War. To his astonishment, he saw his own father's name in the account. The account had listed his father's name and said he had fought bravely and had to have his leg amputated after the battle. The boy stumbled into the other room and asked his mom if the person mentioned in the account was his dad. The mother said yes, but the father had never told the son about it, because his father didn't want his son to think of him as a cripple. The boy realized that the father had used an artificial leg and never talked about it, never used it as a means to get sympathy.

I am a feeler. I want everyone to feel good all the time. I want to please everyone. But I have learned, in the leading of the Spirit, that sometimes the way to freedom for some people is a necessary firmness that may seem harsh. This kind of firmness can only grow out of a real love for the person, and a true hatred of bondage. It is that attitude of bondage that I fight, not the person.

God knows all about the necessity of the inner attitude. He talks about it to his people in Leviticus. They have not made it to the Promised Land. They are still in the desert, and they are still eating a food that they call "what is it?" Yet God has already done something for them, even before they have reached the object of their hope and desire.

"I have broken the bars of your yoke and made you walk erect" (Leviticus 26:13). They have a new attitude even though everything is not perfect. They have a way of walking erect even before the gift of the milk and honey. They have left the attitude of the slave. In recovery groups, sometimes I will ask this Bible question: "When David was homeless and living in a cave, was he any less a king? When Jesus had no place to lay his head and wandered from place to place, was he any less a king?" People usually answer, "No, they were still kings." They were still kings because royalty doesn't depend on circumstances. They were still kings because it is an inside job. It is the attitude of slavery we fight. We have to learn to hate that condition of the mind, because we are slowly becoming like God—true freedom fighters.

principle #2

Limit Your Freedom of Expression — The Prison of Blame

"I have purposed that my mouth shall not transgress. Concerning the works of man, by the word or Your lips I have kept away from the paths of the Destroyer."

PSALM 17:3–4 NKJV

"The search for someone to blame is always successful."

—*Robert Half, businessperson*

Refusing to Bite the Hook

I know that in one sense, what we talked about in the last principle sounds funny. But I have seen it so often—it is important to hate the right thing. The reason we are encouraged to hate evil is because it creates bondage. If we acquiesce to bondage, eventually we become unaware that we are in bondage. This, to me, is the saddest and most permanent bondage of all. Once we are not aware that the bondage around us is bondage, then we set ourselves up for the conditions of a permanent hell, even an eternal hell.

I work with a remarkable man who has taught me so much. He was homeless for periods of his life. He slept on park benches in New York City. He was in and out of mental institutions. He knew that the system was against him because of the color of his skin. It made him furious. He tells of times when he was in a straitjacket, and he was so angry at "the Man" and what had happened to him.

He tells the story of realizing that the outside system wasn't really the essential nature of his bondage. In a sense, he was like that bull that wasted all his energy and strength against the red cape, not realizing the nature of the darts the matador was systematically sinking into his body. Eventually, he came back to Christ and tells the story of his slow process of learning a way to live in health and in wisdom.

He is an anointed teacher. I have sat under his teaching

many times. I have seen him create a space in groups where people can feel free to talk, without hijacking the group. Because of his own experience, people of color feel free to share their heartbreak and the injustices they have encountered. He always listens and allows people to share honestly about their life journey.

However, he was clear that he felt he had learned some things about what the Bible calls "the paths of the Destroyer." After a person had shared all the injustices and difficulties that had made their life a disaster, he would nod his head and reply, "Everything you have said may be true. But if you continue dwelling on those things, it will destroy you. It almost destroyed me."

If someone slipped into an easy kind of dialogue that suggested that the reason things might not be good for the teacher was because of racism, or prejudice against the poor, or some kind of systemic injustice, he would say, "I will not bite that hook. That kind of talk will kill you."

I worked with this teacher day to day. When something difficult came along, or something that seemed impossible, he would say, "I am going to the gym. This thing will train me in patience. Eventually this will make me stronger." This man shared that because of his mental condition. He woke up with intense fear every morning. But he refused to let that fear paralyze him for the day.

I never heard him complain or make excuses, even in small things. He felt as though the problems we encountered were inside jobs. He knew a lot about boxing. Sometimes he would quote to me something that Mike Tyson would say in the early days of his career when he seemed to dominate the boxing world. He said that Tyson made this comment, "I win the victory before I step into the ring." Whenever my co-worker and I would see each other before a day that seemed long and daunting, we would say to each other, "We have already won the victory." It was our code word to each other that the keys to our victory and freedom were not the outside circumstances, but our attitude.

When you associate with anyone like that, their approach becomes contagious. Both of my sons grew up with this teacher in our mission church. His attitude rubbed off on them. The teacher's name was Vaughn, and my sons and I would say we have been "Vaughnitized." Every time someone went into a litany of all the reasons they couldn't do something because of outward circumstances, or every time someone made an excuse for their actions, it sounded so insubstantial to us. "Don't bite that hook," we would say to each other.

I do not want to say what I am saying lightly, for it is very important. I have been working with very difficult situations, people who are homeless, or who have no food, for more than 30 years now. Sometimes the descriptions of the unfairness, or the physical hardships they have had to endure, are overwhelmingly humbling for me. But when I hear the story of all the things that have gone wrong in their life, part of me knows that everyone of those wrongs may be true. But if they continue to dwell on those things, they will never be free.

The self-defeating approach is usually a familiar cocktail of comments—blaming others, providing excuses, giving reasons why they can't do better, making assertions that their current situation is not their fault, wearing self-pity like a scarf.

I know that much of the words spoken are true. Dwelling on this approach continually becomes a killer.

My experience is often with people in visibly horrible circumstances. With people who are chronically in tough circumstances, honestly, I hear the refrain of excuses often. But this approach evinces itself not just with people who might be homeless. If I open my ears, I hear self-justifying excuses in the mansions of the rich as well as with the poor. Apparently, this approach can be an equal-opportunity bondage.

Stating Unfairness Is a Process Not an Address

I need to balance my comments by acknowledging the following: everyone needs to have their story heard. Often, it is more important that we have our story heard than that we get any advice or have any request granted. Recognizing the unfairness of life and what has happened to us can often be an important part of becoming free. Much of my pastoral counseling training has focused on this fact.

However, the script of pointing to what has been done to us can easily become an address, rather than a process. It becomes our script. It becomes the first thing that comes out of our mouths. It becomes our default story whenever we meet new people, or when we are alone. Once this happens, the words become a killer.

Sometimes in our community, we say together that stating the unfairness around us must be part of a process, but it cannot become our address. I personally know of no greater prison than this address.

The address of blame can quickly make a person dependent for life. In my world, I have heard people give all kinds of reasons why they have to drink—because they had a heart condition as a child, because someone in the family treated them horribly, because someone dear to them died long ago. Many of the things they say are true. Sadly, they are not even aware that these reasons have become the prison that keeps them in the same place for life.

Alcoholism in some ways is an easy example. But honestly, the self-justifying urge is quite powerful in all of us. I often consider myself a kind and thoughtful pastor (dream on), and I remember a comment from my teenage son that struck me like a sledgehammer. "Oh, Dad is always right." How sad. I am not always right. But I had shaded my stories and the accounts of my actions to make it look to my son that I was. What an injustice to my poor son. In my conversations with him, I had somehow communicated a mild amnesia to all the totally stupid things I had done in my life. My son's comment woke me up, and helped me not create a bondage I wasn't even aware of.

According to the Bible, blaming others and justifying ourselves is practically our first response when we have done wrong. After sinning, Adam has a nuanced response to God, deflecting all responsibility. It just takes him a few words. God asks, "Have you eaten of the tree which I commanded you not to eat?"

Here is Adam's answer, neatly summarizing what humans continue to do: *"The woman whom you gave to be with me, she gave me fruit of the tree, and I ate"* (Genesis 3:12). Adam is like a maestro of blame, brilliantly instilling so much in his response. In one sentence, Adam makes it God's fault and the woman's fault, without taking any responsibility himself. I sometimes wonder what would have happened if Adam had responded differently, and simply said, "Look, God, I sinned. I take responsibility for what happened. It wasn't Your fault. It wasn't Eve's fault. It was me."

To be honest, we often become experts in this kind of rationalization. Some of us can be very subtle with it. I have been doing it for the last few days, as I was having a theological discussion with a family member. As we talked, my comments became more self-justifying, my memory more slanted in favor of my position, my restating of what I said more complimentary to my own intellect, my refusal to admit any error more intransigent. My vocabulary became larger and larger. Even if I tell a story, I find that I slightly bend the facts, ever so slightly, to favor myself and excuse my behavior. So the story of Adam is not what happened, but what happens. I just love to make a case where it is not my fault.

Certainly this script is not the only one that Satan uses to get us. Of course, Satan is the Hebrew word for the English word *accuser*. Some people go to the other extreme. They are always wrong. If anything goes wrong in any group, they always blame themselves. This is the bondage of blame turned inside out. I suppose that this way is aiming in the right direction, but fatally overshoots the mark.

Our mission church has been involved with tutoring urban children for more than 30 years. One thing I have learned. Our words to children are powerful. Children are learning a "script" for life. What we say to them has far more impact than we realize. Each of us can probably remember things someone said to us as a child. These things brought either damage far out of proportion to the length of the discourse or great life far out of proportion to length of what was said.

The Masters of Blame

The script of blaming others is powerful and deceptive. It is powerful because it can easily become a person's default discourse. It is deceptive because we can so easily become unaware that we are in bondage. The people of God staying in Egypt had apparently been in bondage for centuries. Without realizing it, they seemed to have adopted the language and script of slaves. When Moses starts to work to get them out of Egypt and things don't go well, they blame him. When they are out of Egypt and can't find water, they blame Moses and God. When they feel as though they don't have food, they blame Moses and God and want to return to Egypt. Sometimes they are drama queens and wish they had died in Egypt. They have a PhD in complaining.

We sometimes think complaining and blaming others is a mild thing, an easy convenience that is not really a great problem. Blaming isn't too serious. This approach is a deadly mistake. Finally the people of God get to the Promised Land, the land flowing with milk and honey. They are told there are giants in the land. Their response is such a masterpiece of failing to take responsibility that we need to quote it in full:

> *"Then all the congregation raised a loud cry, and the people wept that night.* [Now, we all know that there is a time to

cry and a time not to cry. Is this the time to cry all night?] *And all the people of Israel grumbled against Moses and Aaron.* [We will learn later how deadly grumbling can be.] *The whole congregation said to them, 'Would that we had died in the land of Egypt! Or would that we had died in this wilderness!* [This is "drama queen (or king)" language. Be careful what you ask for. Their request is eventually granted.] *Why is the LORD bringing us into this land, to fall by the sword? Our wives and our little ones will become a prey.* [Here they blame God and accuse Him of injustice, and they dwell on the worst possible thing that could happen, which incidentally never does.] *Would it not be better for us to go back to Egypt?'* [This is stinking thinking. They have idealized a past that never really was. They are showing remarkable amnesia, forgetting that they were oppressed and remembering minor comforts.] *And they said to one another, 'Let us choose a leader and go back to Egypt'"* (Numbers 14:1–4, bracketed material author's).

As we have said before, this last statement is Pharaoh's ultimate revenge. He is dead, but he has instilled in their minds a self-justification that would lead them back to slavery. It is really not their fault. They need another leader.

What a masterpiece of blaming and complaining. Eventually the people of God, through making complaining their address, get what they ask for. And this fact is often the case for complainers. They never enter the Promised Land, and they die in the wilderness. It is a tragedy that I see on a personal basis almost every day in our missions work.

This kind of blaming can take on a quiet, confidential tone. In Deuteronomy, Moses gives a parting talk to the people of God and reviews their wandering in the wilderness. This is part of what he says about the reason that the people of God did not enter the Promised Land 40 years earlier, when they could have: *"And you murmured in your tents and said, 'Because the*

Lord hated us he has brought us out of the land of Egypt, to give us into the hand of the Amorites, to destroy us'" (Deuteronomy 1:27).

The problem wasn't necessarily always open rebellion. It seemed to have started in a convenient murmuring, not openly, but inside the tents, privately, quietly. It may not have seemed like a big sin, but slowly it became a script. The script focused on the fact that God didn't really love them. As they looked at their circumstances, they refused to see all the good things God had done, and rather focused on the worst part of their circumstances. Then they repeated this as proof that God really didn't like them too much.

It is the same thing the serpent sought to instill in the heart of Adam and Eve. God doesn't have our welfare as His primary concern. If we do not fend for ourselves, dwelling in fear, we will not get the goodies. We rationalize this kind of fear as thoughtful prudence. It is stinking thinking, and eventually, the soft grumbling is not a minor problem. According to Deuteronomy, it keeps us from the Promised Land.

This is the challenge. We gradually recite a script, and eventually plug into a source of fear and accusation. It is not of God. It is of the accuser. And the truth is—the accuser doesn't love us. It is a fatal mistake to take the blaming path of the accuser; it isn't just a few words improperly placed. It isn't just a minor personality trait. You hear it everywhere, once you begin to think about it.

Don't Let It All Out All the Time After All

So what are we to do about this? I have found a fairly straightforward answer. Part of the problem is in the words, and the answer this time is often in the words. We know that death and life are in the power of words (Proverbs 18:21). The way to freedom is the inverse of what we might expect. Oddly, it lies in limiting our freedom of expression rather than expanding our freedom of expression.

As we allow Christ to work in our heart, we find that we are more and more the head and not the tail in our circumstances (Deuteronomy 28:13). My generation promoted the idea that we have to let it out, say what we mean, not limit anything, express your frustrations. There may be a limited truth in some of this, as long as the act is a process and not an address. But the fact of the matter is that sometimes expressing more and more complaints against others engenders more and more bitterness, which can eventually become a killer.

We can learn something from a man who wasn't perfect. In fact, he was a murderer and adulterer. But he was forgiven. His name was David, and he had plenty of opportunities in life to recite a script that focused on blame. "Well, my father really didn't think much of me. When Samuel came to anoint a king, he brought my seven brothers before him, but he didn't even think to call me in. In fact, he kept me out doing the dirty work, being a shepherd. It wasn't fair. Once I began working for Saul, things didn't work out. I did everything right, but Saul hated me. He even tried to murder me. It wasn't fair, and I didn't deserve that. Samuel anointed me king, but that didn't keep me from being homeless. Homeless, I tell you, living in a rotten cave. That wasn't right. Samuel should have told me." You get the idea. David could have painted that kind of picture. But when you read the lyrics of his songs in the Book of Psalms, you hear a narrative of praise and accounts of how a gracious God got David out of one tough experience after another.

He often focuses on his own words. *"I have purposed that my mouth shall not transgress,"* he says in Psalm 17:3. He indicates that by focusing on God's Word, he keeps away from the paths of destroyers (Psalm 17:3–4 NKJV). He wants to be sure that he keeps his lips from speaking lies (Psalm 34:2–14). The greatest lie is that God doesn't have a plan for good for us in the end. He keeps his lips from that by using the replacement theory. *"Let them say continually, let the Lord be magnified"* (Psalm 35:27–28 NKJV). Continually. He is aware of the danger of words that go askew. *"I said, I will take heed to my ways, that I sin not with my tongue. I will keep my mouth with a bridle"* (Psalm 39:1 KJV). He prays to God to help him with his words. *"Set a guard, O Lord, over my mouth; keep watch over the door of my lips!"* (Psalm 141:3). We usually don't pray much about something that isn't an issue for us. I think that controlling the mouth was an issue for David.

The truth of the matter is that we don't have to say everything about everything. Our words are powerful, and we can take heed not to transgress.

For me, we see the process of turning from blame actually happen in one of David's songs. I love these songs because they help me know that we can bring every emotion to God. We see in David, though, how often the emotions we bring undergo a process. In Psalm 139, David ends with vindictive comments about the wicked.

> *"Oh that you would slay the wicked, O God! . . . Do I not hate those who hate you, O Lord? And do I not loathe those who rise up against you? I hate them with a complete hatred; I count them my enemies"* (vv. 19–22).

Sounds pretty much as though the hatred is focused on people and that it is all their fault.

But look at the shift in the final part of the song. It is almost as if we can watch the change from blame to taking responsibility. *"Search me, O God, and know my heart! Try me and know my thoughts! And see if there be any grievous way in me, and lead me in the way everlasting"* (vv. 23–24). What a change, and for me, what a move toward freedom, forgetting about hatred and blame, and moving toward self-analysis and being open to change in himself.

With God's grace, we do have the power to replace words of blame with words of power. My co-worker taught me through his own hard circumstances that it isn't really about what others did to you. This fact is one of the greatest freedoms we can see in light.

Clearly Jesus was not afraid to talk. He was a great storyteller. He spent a lot of time in dialogue in the temple and at the synagogues. He was such a good talker that people remembered what He said and eventually wrote it down. But when He had been arrested and brought to a kangaroo court in the middle of the night, they brought all kinds of blame on Him. Crazy things, murderous things, false things. Surely He would open his mouth to defend himself, to justify His circumstances, to retell the story in a favorable light. But the Bible says He remained silent in the midst of all that blame (Mark 14:61). I wonder what that felt like.

principle #3
Narrow Your Focus—The Prison of Family Anger

"Love does not rejoice with wrongdoing."

1 CORINTHIANS 13:6

"Anybody can become angry—that is easy, but to be angry with the right person and to the right degree and at the right time and for the right purpose, and in the right way—that is not within everybody's power and is not easy."

—*Aristotle*

Turning Out the Lights

*M*anny (short for Emmanuel, "God is with us") curled his upper lip into a sneer at the mention of the subject. I had known him for years. He would come by to get a lunch or some clothes from time to time. He was always courteous to me. He was smart. He was able-bodied. People on the street seemed to like him. He was always talking about what he was going to do and how he was going to get out of his current situation.

He and I were looking at options together at the moment. I hadn't mentioned anything that I thought was hateful, but I had learned to recognize that look. I had mentioned his family. Apparently his brother had told his cousin Manny was stupid, and he wasn't talking to his sister. They had a fight over the death of his mother, and his uncle wouldn't let him stay over when he was in a jam. His face hardened. His anger at his family became the reason he wasn't looking for a job or couldn't find a place to stay. His anger was a prison.

I do not want to treat family anger lightly. I have seen it in many circumstances, and I know how deep it can go and how hard it is to deal with. Lawyers and pastors know what the funeral of someone with resources can do to a family. It goes deeper than that. Abuse, neglect, violence, the warping of a person, the mind cage created by an oppressive script, the feeling of being ignored—they all get caught up in the family emotions. Being around family can make a person into a walking volcano. Anyone who is gripped by it knows that it can feel like a prison that one can never escape. It is easy for someone to tell you what you ought to do or ought to feel, but the chains only feel heavier because you now feel guilty for not being able to get beyond the anger.

I cannot point my finger at Manny. I have known the grip of hardly being able to speak in some extended family situations because of unresolved anger. In our church, I have seen older people continue to be controlled by anger about some other person, 20 years after the person has died.

I have seen countless people who have been gripped by family anger to the degree that they don't function. They self-medicate, they become homeless, and worst of all, they repeat the same wrongs on someone else in their own life. This is an insidious mind cage that keeps on persecuting to the third and fourth generations. I hate it.

We often say at the mission that anger is like drinking poison and expecting the other person to die. It is a killer. One fumes over a toxic cocktail of anger and bitterness and thoughts about what one should have done. We have read the medical studies that some diseases may be connected to anger. I read recently that the preface to Uzziah's leprosy was a prideful anger (2 Chronicles 26:19). I have noticed that the few times I have been very sick have also been times I have harbored and nurtured anger within.

God is a freedom fighter. He does not want us bound, and He does not want us to be in that loneliness, cut off from family. *"He sets the solitary in families, and brings those who are bound into prosperity"* (Psalm 68:6 NKJV). He wants those who are imprisoned to be free.

Here is the prison of unawareness working so acutely. I have had times when I felt my righteous indignation and anger at a person was so justified, that I could not see clearly. Without realizing it, the anger became a hatred, a hatred that I felt was correct. I did not realize that I was doing the same thing that 1 John 2:11 talked about. I was in darkness and walked in darkness and didn't know where I was going because the darkness had blinded my eyes.

When we started our mission, the youth always wanted to play a particular game. The game involved turning the lights completely out and trying to find the other person. You can imagine the problems this little game eventually involved—running into chairs in the dark, tripping over tables, bashing your face in an unexpected door. We had to ban the game because it was so clearly injurious.

Turning out the light before you walk across a room is obviously stupid. I did it last night as I stayed in a motel room. I walked across the room at night without turning the lights on and banged both of my shins badly. I would have been even more stupid if I had tried to run across the room.

Once I have visualized how obtuse I would be to do such an act, I have begun to realize how foolish I am when I move from personal anger to the beginnings of hatred. It is like turning out the lights. I may be convinced that finally, I am really seeing the other person clearly for who he or she is, but according to the Bible, I am not. Hatred blinds my eyes, and more likely than not, I am liable to do something idiotic, which will end up banging up my own person.

Choose Something Else On the Menu

A revelation comes when we realize that we have a choice in the matter. It is liberating to realize that I cannot control what my family does to me, but I can control how I respond to them. When we refuse the path of hatred and choose a path to love in a real way, not some fluffy, fearful way, we take the path of rightness. This is what the Bible says about the path of the ones who choose rightness: *"But the path of the righteous is like the light of dawn, which shines brighter and brighter until full day"* (Proverbs 4:18).

I have seen this happen many times. When a person chooses to take a step from hatred, the path, ever so subtly, reveals a little bit more light. As a person moves toward choosing a way that is not hateful, he or she will eventually have a moment of seeing a different path. It will experientially "dawn" on them.

I also see what keeps many people from even considering doing so. The other family member has been so destructive, so hurtful, so abusive to the victim's most vulnerable areas that the person refuses to even consider a change of attitude. At first, it sounds as though the other family member might interpret any change in attitude as an opportunity to just walk all over the victim again. In group times, I have often had to say, "We are not called to be a doormat."

This is the way I say it in our group: "If a parent abused you as a child, you can forgive them, but that doesn't mean you have to let them babysit your children." Clearly, part of love is learning appropriate boundaries, learning when to say no. Eric Liddell, the real-life protagonist in the movie *Chariots of Fire*, once wrote a study on the Sermon on the Mount. I remember reading about his comments long ago. As I remember, he said that this is his distinction between weak and meek. According to Liddell, weak is kind and gentle and full of fear. Meek is kind and gentle and fearless. Being released from family anger and hatred does not mean giving into fearfulness. It means being kind and fearless and setting boundaries that need to be set.

You never know what will help you get to the point of release. Sometimes the family anger has become so imbedded in who we are that we don't know where to begin. We sometimes have to pray that God will help us want to want to forgive. I found help in an example from a TV preacher. He said that he hated curry. When he went to an Indian restaurant with his family, he found that almost everything on the menu had curry. However, he refused to let that fact ruin his time with his family. He said he would find the one dish that did not have curry, and focus on that.

In the same manner, sometimes the apparent abundance of bad qualities in a family member seems to take up the whole menu. Then those bad qualities threaten to ruin the entire time with family. But like the preacher, we can choose to focus on the one good quality in that family member, and still enjoy the family time. If we think about it seriously, we can usually find that one good quality somewhere.

Paul, who seemed to have been in every jail in the Mediterranean, knew a thing or two about being in physical bondage. However, he had a key to liberation when he talked about choosing love. He said that, *"love does not rejoice at wrongdoing, but rejoices with the truth"* (1 Corinthians 13:6).

We can focus on the one thing that aims at goodness and truth in the other person. It is this practice that can bring liberation in our family. Often, we find ourselves in the other camp — rejoicing in the wrongdoing, taking pleasure in reciting to all who will listen concerning the sad nature of a particular family member. Eventually we become a gossip, and then an accuser, and finally we have built a wall of condemnation around ourselves. Thinking the wall of condemnation is a defense, it becomes a prison. Usually we know deep in our hearts that we have not completely lived up to the standard we are applying to the other person. In the end, it really is a bit like being in jail.

More Like a Flute Than an Onion

*H*ere is the freedom key, I believe, and it works with all the prisons, in one way or other. It can help the incarcerated person become the uncarcerated. The world can seem like a swamp of confusing, moral choices, especially within our own family. Here, however, is the way to discern what to do. Paul makes it simple. He says simply, *"walk in love"* (Ephesians 5:2). In every circumstance, we are to think what the path of love would be. John, who was also known to have been a prisoner on the Island of Patmos, has another way to say the same thing. He says that once we know and believe the love God has for us, we can "abide" in love. *"God is love, and whoever abides in love abides in God, and God abides in him"* (1 John 4:16).

Here is the love manifesto with Paul. It is also the way to liberation with families.

> *"Love is patient and kind; Love does not envy or boast. It is not arrogant or rude. It does not insist on its own way. It is not irritable or resentful. It does not rejoice in the wrongdoing, but rejoices with the truth. Love bears all things, believes all things, hopes all things, endures all things. Love never ends"* (1 Corinthians 13:4–8).

If you read this passage through, chances are something will leap out at you and you will know it is the area the Holy Spirit is working on (my area right now happens to be the "irritable and resentful" part). We are not alone as we take this path. From what I can gather from the biblical accounts, I am not sure that Paul was naturally all that loving. He seems to be a bit of an irascible character once or twice in Acts (23:3–4), and in defending his apostleship, he doesn't hesitate to move to a bit of sarcasm in 2 Corinthians. Paul is a fellow traveler with us too.

Furthermore, we have a promise. In the end, I don't think we are so much like an onion, with more and more layers as we get to a core. I think we are more like a flute. We need the breath of the Musician flowing through us to become what we were made to be. Here is how Paul describes it before he comes to the place of his most notorious captivity: *"God's love has been poured into our hearts through the Holy Spirit who has been given unto us"* (Romans 5:5). Like many things in the New Testament, love is two things. It is something we do, and it is something given to us. So we know this path of love is the freedom road, and we know we do not do it on our own. We have the Spirit breath flowing through us.

Sometimes, we think that by having the freedom to hate a person, we become fully liberated. It is a snare. Even popular movies know this sometimes. In *Star Wars*, every time Luke Skywalker strikes out in anger, doesn't Darth Vader say something like, "Good, connect with the dark side of the force"? Even Hollywood suspects that in the end, this kind of hatred doesn't really bring the freedom it promises, though Hollywood continues to make a lot of money capitalizing on retaliation and revenge stories.

We sometimes turn to Joseph in Genesis as the poster child for family abuse. Joseph gets it. Some of his brothers talk about killing him. He is in bondage because of his family. He is a slave because of them. He is a prisoner. He is forgotten. What a wonderful movie of revenge we could make of his story, once he becomes one of the most powerful men in the world, and his conniving brothers don't even know he is alive. We could watch with pleasure as he gives exquisite, tortuous punishment to each one—what a wonderful slasher movie it could be.

Yet Joseph makes the upside-down choice to freedom. Instead of exercising his power, he moves toward another response. He is not naive anymore. He doesn't reveal himself immediately, and sets up some hurdles for his brothers to pass. Yet in the end, he chooses another way to view his family. *"As for you, you meant evil against me, but God meant it for good"* (Genesis 50:20). Once he makes that choice, he truly becomes uncarcerated.

principle #4

Enjoy Stone Barriers — The Prison of Attitude

"Rejoice in the Lord always; again I will say, rejoice."

PHILIPPIANS 4:4; PAUL IN JAIL

"When you can't stay out of the storm, the storm must stay out of you."

—*a radio preacher*

Two More Jailbirds

*G*et ready. This may be the most important chapter. It is certainly going to sound like a contradiction to principle #1—learn to hate. But that is OK. As we grow older, we see more clearly that in some ways the world is full of paradoxical truths—truths that seem contradictory but must be put side by side in order to understand reality. Some scientists have had to come to terms with this experience. As we mentioned in the introduction, Niels Bohr was a quantum physicist who understood that light functioned both as a wave and as a particle, and that these two seemingly opposing truths needed to be held simultaneously. He is often quoted as saying that the opposite of a profound truth is another profound truth. Furthermore, Martin Luther and other biblical reformers, as they delved deeply again into the Word of God, saw that many of the truths of God functioned the same way. So here we go as we think about freedom.

I wish we talked about Boethius more in our current times. Apparently, they loved him in the Middle Ages and his thought was very influential. He was a kind of Christian philosopher in the early sixth century. One could argue about his combination of Christianity and philosophy all day, but the context in which he wrote is compelling.

Being involved with the administration of the Roman government, he held high positions and was greatly respected.

Then there came a time when he fell out of favor with the king. He found himself in prison. He became bitter in thinking about the wavering nature of the populace, their fickleness and lack of loyalty. He thought about the way his generous and unselfish actions had been reinterpreted as self-serving and ill-advised. In short, his life was the pits.

He wrote a book about his experiences called *The Consolation of Philosophy*. In it, Philosophy, personified as a lady, comes to him and seems to berate him. He has gotten so caught up in his own troubles that he has forgotten what Philosophy has taught him. She teaches him again. One of the concepts is, pardon the expression, the "wheel of fortune." We accept in life that sometimes things go up and sometimes they go down, just like a wheel. Once we accept this, we are not disappointed by failure, nor deceived by success. In his book, Boethius becomes uncarcerated. Like Paul, he is eventually executed.

This concept of the turning of the wheel was very important in some of the art of medieval times. For 1,000 years after his death, the writing of Boethius helped people come to terms with what was happening to him. Even in prison, in the worst of circumstances, we can be at peace. We are not deceived by the wheel of fortune.

Isn't it strange that even though this idea is so obvious, we seem to forget it in our current lives? We are emotionally devastated when things go bad and unrealistically elated if the wheel of fortune goes up. The idea of this kind of inner contentment has gone out of vogue. It is the sign of the banality of our times that the phrase connected with Boethius only seems to remain as the title of a still-popular game show on TV.

Boethius documents his own profound change of attitude, from bitterness and self-pity, to a kind of serenity. He came to understand that his freedom was an inside job. His freedom, in the end, did not depend on circumstances.

Another poster child of the uncarcerated could be Richard Lovelace, because outside of Paul (we will get to him), Lovelace gave us our most memorable phrase concerning upside-down freedom. Lovelace was a dashing, long-haired poet in seventeenth-century England, and I would imagine that he was no "saint" in our conventional conceptions. As a supporter of the king in changing times in England, he found himself in prison on more than one occasion. While in prison, he wrote a poem, perhaps to his girlfriend ("To Althea From Prison"). The poem ends with these lines:

> Stone walls do not a prison make,
> Nor iron bars a cage;
> Minds innocent and quiet take
> That for an Hermitage;
> If I have freedom in my Love,
> And in my soul am free;
> Angels alone that soar above,
> Enjoy such Liberty.

My boys learned these lines as young children. I wish every child would (forgive me, I was an English major). I think they have very practical implications for our lives. Even today, when circumstances seem difficult, our family makes this shorthand statement, "Stone walls do not a prison make." It all depends on how you look at things. Once we change our view, we could see the same confinement as a place of prayer, the kind of place that people at one time sought out as a place for reflection. It could be an opportunity for making the connection with God.

In some ways, Lovelace was able to turn the tables on his oppressors. They thought they were punishing him, but he chose to see the very walls as signs of a liberty that rivals the liberty of angels. He chose to look at those very walls in a different way. He chose to channel his confinement into something memorable—a poem. Incidentally, this poem doesn't point to a necessarily rosy future. Despite Lovelace's charm and good looks, his life continued to have serious storms. He died before he was 40, living on charity, destitute and forgotten.

Loving the Iron Knob

Peter, no stranger to jails himself, says that we are to add virtue to faith (2 Peter 1:5). Virtue, to me, is acting like a hero when no one is looking. It is developing the strength to refuse to allow the circumstances to define who we are. *Virtue* is an out-of-date word, but I think we need to resurrect it, to add strength to our faith. Virtue reminds us of the value of responding with backbone instead of responding like an amoeba, allowing ourselves to be molded by everything that seems difficult.

The quality that Lovelace probes is the act of actually reversing our view of the oppressive bonds, of seeing them as a help rather than a hindrance. G. K. Chesterton writes a wonderful book called *The Ball and the Cross* (I had to read it twice to like it). One of the characters is Father Michael, and for me, he is yet another upside-down freedom character. He is an odd person, who seems quite simple and childish on first acquaintance. He accompanies a believer and an atheist through a number of zany adventures; but as the story proceeds, we begin to suspect that though Father Michael seems very childlike to the "wiser" people in the story. He seems to touch on something transcendent, something beyond our normal seeing, and something deeper, closer to what reality really is.

At one point, the protagonists find themselves in, you guessed it, an asylum that is really like a prison (seems to be the theme in this chapter). One of the characters sees an iron peg protruding from the wall of his prison. He finds it ugly and annoying. He can see no purpose for its existence. It tends to infuriate him, a mild, protruding, useless piece of iron. The peg works on his brain like Chinese water torture until he goes practically insane. It seems to him like the most insidious kind of persecution.

We find out later that Father Michael, in the same circumstances, not only endures the presence of this iron knob. Father Michael loves the knob. It's his favorite thing in the room. In terms of the context of the story, we realize that this seemingly extraneous incident becomes a linchpin for the whole book. Father Michael, in his childlike ways, is able to bring God, who is love, into the everyday little annoyances of life. His love transforms the prison into an enjoyment. He finds a way to enjoy the thing that is breaking the spirit of the other inmates.

Here is a key. Sometimes we can turn the tables on bondage by enjoying the barriers. We can refuse to let circumstances become the defining guides in our soul. This will seem repulsive to some. As Robert Frost says, "Something there is that doesn't love a wall." Surely, as we said in principle #1, we sometimes need to learn to hate the binding mind cages in our lives. The other part of that hatred is realizing that even if we have an outward cage, we do not have to allow it to enslave us.

Father Michael's strange approach can make us think. There is something about enjoyment which we know, deep down, is the heart of life. While he is on the run, David tells us to taste and see that the Lord is good (Psalm 34:8). God, according to David, gives us drink from the river of His pleasures (Psalm 36:8). Even as we enjoy God, we learn that

He is not utterly pleased until we are utterly pleased. Dorothy Day, the writer and activist, worked many years serving the poor in my neighborhood. As she grew older, she had a wonderful phrase. She said that we need to cultivate "the duty of delight." Even in the dirtiness and smell of serving those who were in difficult situations, one could find ways to enjoy something there—a flower on the table, a joke from someone eating a meal.

Artists know this, and you see it all over the place. Sometimes, when things are difficult, it is the practice of enjoying something there that turns the tide for our hearts. Larry McMurtry, in *Lonesome Dove*, writes about a classic character, Augustus McCrae. Gus is no conventional Christian by a long shot, though we are told he reads the Bible in the morning and serves as a kind of pastor to the group of men driving the cattle. At one point, he makes this comment: "If you want one thing too much, it's likely to be a disappointment. The healthy way is to learn to like the everyday things."

I saw the movie *Dr. Zhivago* a long time ago, and for a long time, I could only remember one scene in the movie. Dr. Zhivago, a doctor who is also a poet, is being transported in crowded, horrible conditions in a boxcar. He can remember his earlier privileged life, and everything around him seems hellish. However, he is able to open up the tiniest of windows from his sleeping mat in the boxcar, really a vent. Through the vent, he is able to feast on the view of the snow in the night. He drinks in the beauty and is happy.

When I was in Hong Kong, I heard an Eastern story that has shaped my life. It doesn't have a punch line, but imbedded in the little story is a key to freedom. Here is the story as I remember it: A tiger is chasing a man. The man comes to a cliff with the tiger behind him. He is trapped. He sees a rope hanging down from the cliff. In order to get away from the tiger, he climbs down the rope. He gets to the end of the rope.

He is still a long way from the bottom. Holding on, he looks down. There are deadly jagged rocks beneath him. He looks up just above where his hands are holding the rope. A mouse is on the rope nibbling through the threads. The man looks across him to the cliff. A small cluster of wild strawberries are growing there. He reaches out with one hand and plucks some and puts them into his mouth. He says, "These strawberries are delicious."

I told you there was no punch line. The point of the story to me is that we will always have a hungry tiger behind us. And we always have jagged rocks ahead of us. And at the present, we will always have a mouse nibbling at the rope just above our hands. But the key in life is to be able to reach out to the "strawberries" in those circumstances, and say, "These strawberries are delicious."

This is another code sentence in my family. When things seem tough or horrible, we can stop at lunch, look at each other, and say, "These strawberries are delicious." Sometimes that is about all we can do.

I believe that David, who knew what it was to be a fugitive and to have many enemies, knew the secret to this. That is why he makes the astonishing statement in Psalm 23: "You prepare a table before me in the presence of my enemies." I love that picture, with David enjoying a feast while his enemies are all around him. It is a truth of freedom we need to relearn. If we must wait until there are no enemies, we will miss a lot of the feast of life.

Ethical Jujitsu

Facing the world this way can bring a kind of jujitsu on oppression. If jujitsu takes the force of the opponent and goes with it until the opponent is overthrown, then taking the captor's instructions and going with it might mean a kind of victory. When I was a teenager, I loved a movie called *Cool Hand Luke*, which was about a chain gang in the 1930s. At one point, the chain gang was forced to do a very tiring job on a hot day of throwing asphalt on a road. No one wanted to do it, and it was going to be a grueling day. Cool Hand Luke (Paul Newman) decided to take the instructions into overdrive. He got all the men to hustle and act as though it was fun. Before they knew it, as the guards got more flustered because their commands were being followed so closely, the work began to feel like fun. They finished the job super quickly. Then they got to rest, because those who were to pick them up never anticipated their action. Here was for me an example of a different way to respond to oppressive circumstances. The different way involved making what was supposed to be punishing into something enjoyable. Jujitsu takes the force of the opponent, goes with it, until there is an unexpected outcome. It's one way to freedom.

Jesus had a feel for that kind of liberation. He lived in a colony. The overlords could do a humiliating thing. They could tap a person and the person was required by law to carry their goods a mile. Think of the bitterness as you watched a family member taken from their business to do a service for the Roman soldier who had violently conquered your country. But Jesus turns the tables in His own way. Volunteer to go another mile, He says. Think of the conversations such an action would provoke on that 20-minute extra walk. In a way, the victim of oppression has taken back the freedom of choice by choosing to do more for a soldier. Ethical jujitsu.

Once we begin to think of it, this kind of choice goes on all the time in the New Testament. Paul and Silas, beaten, exhausted, placed in the worst part of the prison late at night in Philippi, could have bickered with each other, or at best, met their bad fortune with glum silence. They didn't do it. Instead, we find them singing praises (Acts 16:25–26).

We see what often happens, in some form or other. The prison walls crumble. Freedom.

Thanking God When Something Stinks

*I*ronically, in an inverse manner, praise and thankfulness in the midst of the most oppressive barriers tend to make walls come down. Paul, that constant prisoner, understands this as he says to be thankful in all circumstances in 1 Thessalonians 5:18. Paul goes even further in Ephesians 5:20. He leaves no doubt in his instructions: *"Giving thanks always and for everything."* I used to say I will thank God *in* all circumstances but not *for* all circumstances. We know that God hates oppression. But we also learn a deeper truth. God is so awesome, such a freedom fighter, that in the end, He will take even horrible circumstances and bring good out of them (Romans 8:28). This deep truth is an amazing chain-breaker.

I am often told by those who are a part of Alcoholics Anonymous that the attitude of gratitude is a key element in survival. It is not just some nice frosting on the cake when things go well. By stopping and remembering to be thankful in tough circumstances, one can live another day. Thankfulness helps a person reframe his or her life. It is reframing how we look at things. I love the AA saying: "The pain you feel is not the arrow going in; it is the arrow going out."

I have found four times where Jesus says thank you. Surprisingly, none of the times are times when things are going particularly well. One time is when Jesus doesn't have any tangible evidence of sufficient resources. He only has five hamburger buns and two sardines, and He has thousands to feed. The Bible says that Jesus took those pathetically miniscule resources and gave thanks for them (John 6:11). Probably not the kind of prayer I would have started with. I tend to think that desperate, anxiety-filled pleading is the way to reach God.

Another time, Jesus has just had a very tough time in ministry. Things are not working out the way He had hoped. He has to recite a series of "woes" on all the cities that have refused to respond to His ministry, who have refused to repent. But in the middle of these "woes," Jesus says this: *"I thank you, Father, Lord of heaven and earth, that you have hidden these things from the wise and understanding and revealed them to little children."* Clearly Jesus' disciples were not always the brightest crayons in the box, which could have been another reason to get glum and frustrated. But when Jesus has a tough time in ministry, He thanks God for the co-workers with Him, no matter how flawed they might seem sometimes (Matthew 11:25).

A third time Jesus thanks God is when things stink. Literally. Jesus is facing an impossible situation. He has arrived late, which has bothered some, and Lazarus has died. When Jesus says to roll away the tombstone, Martha reminds Him that Lazarus will smell bad because he has been dead four days. In this stinking, impossible situation, Jesus starts His prayer by thanking God, giving thanks because the Father has heard Him (John 11:41). Thanksgiving seems to be an important part of breaking even the strongest physical bonds, the bonds of death.

Finally, Jesus gives thanks when one of His closest friends stabs Him in the back. Even when He is eating with the man who He knows has already betrayed Him, He stops to thank God for the food they are going to eat (Luke 22:17–19).

This is a lot of Scripture, so let's get practical. In the toughest circumstances is the time that Jesus gives thanks. Thanking God seems to activate the workings of faith in the hardest times. I have seen this attitude of thankfulness become the road to freedom for so many people. Finding good in the toughest times seems to turn the tables on our bondage.

Being thankful for tough things is an upside-down way to freedom, and it doesn't make sense. As we have mentioned, God could either bless us by having us never encounter problems, or bless us by helping us grow so that regardless of the circumstances, we are free. It seems that given our circumstances, God has chosen the second way.

James, the brother of Jesus, got it. He says, *"Count it all joy, brothers and sisters, when you meet trials of various kinds."* (James 1:2). What? That sounds like advice from a nutjob. But, James gives the reason. "For you know that the testing of your faith produces steadfastness." This is what the Lord is looking for—virtue. God has a purpose. *"And let steadfastness have its full effect, that you may be perfect and complete, lacking nothing."* There it is—the result. It sounds great. Perfect and complete, lacking nothing (James 1:3–4). Nothing can stop us. It is an inside job. "Stone walls do not a prison make."

principle #5
Build Walls — The Prison of Cultural Expectations

"You shall have no other gods before me."

EXODUS 20:3

"I'll not deny we should be glad to have you for a bit. You see, we're not used to such troubles; and the Rangers have all gone away, folk tell me. I don't think we've rightly understood till now what they did for us."

—Mr. Butterbur in J. R. R. Tolkien's
Lord of the Rings

A Missionary Drowned by Gold

This is the toughest chapter for me to write yet. The reason it is so difficult is that the views go against much of prevailing sentiment. It is important for us to read and to think in a longer view, including what we know of our history. Otherwise, we start thinking all the issues we are facing are new issues, that the issues raised are literally a "new deal." Often practices have been tried in many societies in many times and in many ways. It is really not all that new. I have a friend who sometimes says, "This is not new. It is just new to you."

Idolatry is a word we don't use anymore. It sounds so ominous, so old-school, so priggish. But for our purposes it is a very important word. In one sense, it does mean anything that takes the place of God. But for me, as I look at it, it is any false way to freedom. It is Pinocchio going to Pleasure Island. It is the prodigal son running away from his dad with all his new money. It is 1,000 people I have met who came to the city to find liberty. It is the rich person trapped, alone and bored, in his depressing mansion.

God hates idolatry. Part of the reason He hates it is because it doesn't lead to freedom, and as we keep saying, God is a freedom fighter. To me, the emphasis prohibiting idolatry is not some barbaric vestige of a primitive religion. It is simply practical. The other ways to freedom just don't work.

This is part of the reason the Exodus story, the story of people moving from slavery to freedom, is so important. God gets the slaves out of bondage, but it is clear from the constant complaining and grumbling about what has happened, that the slaves still have a long way to go. Don't we all.

At one point, not long after they have been so miraculously delivered, God gives them ten instructions, or commandments (Exodus 20). Some of the commandments sound like prohibitions, or barriers. The first one states that the people should have no other gods before them. My son often points out that in a sense all the Ten Commandments are about idolatry. Coveting is thinking that something else will fill the place that only God can fill. Stealing is thinking some material object is more important than other people or God. Forgetting the Sabbath is making our work our God. In each of these instances, we see that God wants freedom for us so that we will not be cramped or deluded by some illusion of real freedom.

Every group of people have to deal with idolatry. We often have other names for it. As we read history, we see that different generations have different issues pressing in on them, things that seem so horribly important to them at the time. For example, we address the issues of "graven images" differently now than in Old Testament times. The challenges of human sacrifice, which were prevalent in a number of cultures around Israel at some periods of Old Testament times, are different now, and take different forms.

Looking at other ages, sometimes we can see their problems more clearly than we can see our own. We recognize the mechanics of their problems, but we are obtuse concerning our own idolatry. The idolatry is too ingrained in our lives. For example, if people were learning another language, they might be very aware of the grammar involved in that language. Yet they don't think about the grammar they use in their own language every day, because it is just second nature to them.

So let's state one of the false ways to freedom that is culturally very strong in our time—thinking that money will make us comfortable and that having it is a legitimate goal for life. That is the American aim, as Francis Schaeffer, the Christian writer, put it so long ago—personal peace and affluence. Our culture assumes that this is a legitimate, ultimate goal for life. But it doesn't really work. It's not enough.

We tend to imagine that idolatry means some primitive people (not us) bowing down before some totem of a bull or an owl or something. However, even in the Bible, in an age where those kinds of images are much more prevalent, idolatry is a much wider term. Paul, during a time he is in prison once again, writes about bondage in his letter to the Ephesians. He gives them a number of instructions, and among other things, he says, *"that everyone who is sexually immoral or impure, or who is covetous (that is, an idolater) has no inheritance in the kingdom of Christ and God"* (5:5). According to Paul, this yearning for other things we do not have, this intangible covetousness, is a form of idolatry.

We know this fact in our heart. It would be unkind to list the rich and famous people who have so much wealth and who seem so unhappy, overdosing on drugs, attempting suicide, choosing destructive patterns and people. It is on the news every night. It is a cliché.

Recently our family got together, and we were remembering the stories my mother told us about growing up as the daughter of a medical missionary to China. She told of a missionary in China who drowned traveling down the river. The boat overturned, and in that day before credit cards and secure banking systems, the missionary was carrying significant amounts of gold and silver concealed in his coat pockets for his travels and the missions. The weight of his clothes was too secure and diverse for him, and he sank and died.

In my mother's eyes, this story was a parable of what an attachment to gold can do to you—make you sink. I am so thankful that God has promised He has plans for peace and prosperity for us (Jeremiah 29:11). My wife often says that money is a power, but it is a low form of power. For me, the danger of money is the accompanying cultural expectations. As we grow older and accumulate money, it creates the illusion that we are making progress. We have enough to get a bigger house or have more financial security, and we forget to see if we are growing in faith, hope, and love on the inside. And as we keep seeing when we think about freedom, it is really an inside job.

The cultural expectation is so powerful, that we are often unable to set a boundary, to build a wall around how much we receive. I remember reading about an author who had a hugely successful book. He was giving much of his royalties away. He made an interesting comment during a TV interview about the way he was dispensing his new wealth. He simply said this: you can really only have so much molasses. There is no sense piling up barrel after barrel of molasses—it won't help you. He saw money that way. You only needed so much. Having more is like trying to eat too much cheesecake.

Can any of us deny the difficulty of setting the boundaries on money? We get a bit extra and we begin to feel that if we can just get this certain item, whether it is a cigar or an airplane, then everything will be alright on the deepest levels of our being.

Hoarders on Every Level

*M*any ages and societies have had to deal with these issues, and we certainly see it in the Bible. In some ways, Ecclesiastes is the story of the man who had it all, and he sees it isn't enough. How sad to see Solomon as he looks at those who will inherit the fruits of all his work, and he sees the abuse and dissipation that comes about in succeeding generations. When we see the dreary sadness in the children of successful people, or in their children's children, we know that the story is still being played out.

We can also understand in a new way how severe Moses is when he sees that the people have made a calf, out of gold no less, to worship. Moses takes the golden calf and grinds it up and scatters it in the water and makes the people drink it (Exodus 32:20). Some people think that Moses made them drink it so that the next day he could point to their urine and say, "There is your god."

Earlier in our work in the Lower East Side, we encountered a number of people who tended to hoard things. Sometimes their apartments were filled to the ceiling, and they were about to get evicted, but they still could not let go. I don't pretend to understand all the dynamics involved with this challenge. However, I have seen in myself, when we as a family had less money, I tended to keep things. I kept things because

I thought, *I may never come across this item again, and I don't have enough to buy another.* I tended to hoard out of a sense of want.

During that time, my wife and I visited a friend who was very rich. Her house was immaculate. All her closets were clean with lots of room. I realized that she could easily throw things away. She could always get another one. It didn't matter. She was rich.

I heard an African pastor quoted as saying, "True wealth is getting just what you need at just the right time from the proper Source." He didn't have to worry or try to hoard.

Some of our idolatry of money comes from forgetting our true source. We may not fill up our house with junk, but we hoard it in our heart. Still, the hoarding is a trap that crowds out the place for ourselves or for God. Like the other things we have talked about, money is an inside job. Working in the inner city, I have seen people who have very little, but who live richly. One man used to say, "I am houseless, but not homeless." In the same vicinity, I have also seen people who have a lot of money, but they act like paupers, with faces drawn and angry. Wealth can be a wonderful thing, and our ministry has given us the chance to work with many decent people with the gift of giving. However, I live close enough to the centers of money in Manhattan to know that some people are worshipping their god with 80 hours at work a week. They are eventually going to be humiliated by the insignificance of what they are serving.

We must set up a wall, a boundary, against the onslaught of expectation that getting more things and more comfort is the point of life. God isn't being unkind to us when He gives us these instructions. He just doesn't want us to fall into the trap. We can see how unhappy other people become serving this god. It is just so much harder for us to see it when it is happening to us.

Smaller and Dingier and More Promiscuous

*L*ack of boundaries in sexual ethics is another false way to freedom. We have all seen the sad cases where someone thought they were pursuing personal freedom in their sexual activity, and in the end, they wound up lonely and empty, a two-dimensional person focusing on personal needs. This issue is hard to discuss because we have so much emotional investment in what we have done or plan to do. I don't think it is unfair to point out the obvious, that huge amounts of artistic energy and resources have been poured out to make sexual commitment to one person look stodgy and unliberated. Turn on the TV, go to the movies, listen to some music. We have gotten to the point that to say anything different than the prevailing view sounds oppressive. It's not the first time that these circumstances have happened in history.

When someone tells me things in society have changed, and that we are at a new stage in civilization, I sometimes ask them to read a small work by Petronius called *Satyricon*. Petronius was a friend of Nero's in the AD 50s. He was known as the "arbiter of elegance," which I suppose is sort of like saying "the duke of cool," or something similar. For me, *Satyricon* is a breezy, mocking account of life in the city, where anything goes sexually. In the end, everyone ends up using everyone else, and it is supposed to be amusing, I suppose, in a "sophisticated" way.

Some of Paul's letters were written at about the same time as Petronius's clever work. The next time we read Paul's letters to the troubled Corinthian church, with its injunction to abstain from sexual immorality and aim for purity, we must remember that Paul was writing in a time when the force of wealth and power in society had a very different view of the range of sexual norms. The halls of power supported it. We've forgotten that at the time Paul was writing, the emperor Nero had his boyfriend dress for a wedding and married him.

Because sexual relationships are so powerful (and from a Christian view, so absolutely wonderful), it is worthwhile to take some time to think deeply about them. We all know the dangers. My generation proclaimed a liberating sexual revolution, but pastors and counselors have since picked up the pieces of the children of that revolution. To be honest, there have been a lot of casualties from the inconsistency, betrayal, adultery, multiple partners, and self-centeredness of my generation. Our children took a lot of the hits. I know the pitch that is given in the push of the prevailing media, that this was all a movement toward freedom. My experience as a pastor has taught me that whenever there are sexual relations outside of marriage, people forget the shrapnel that is entailed. One partner may think no one is hurt, but often the other partner may feel great hurt. If not the couple, then the children. If not the children, then the extended family. If not the extended family, then the close friends. The long-term consequences can be immense, all the way, as the Bible so aptly says it, to the third and fourth generation.

Again we see the strange paradox of freedom. We think we are choosing the way that transcends the boundaries, that in our case things are different, that we will find greater freedom. After a while, the freedom we think we have achieved becomes tawdry. The same issues we fled emerge again, perhaps in a different form. The new love, who we thought would change everything, turns out to have his or her own issues.

Again, these challenges are not new. My wife has just finished reading a novel called *The Age of Innocence* by Edith Wharton. It was published in 1920. In it, a gentleman who sees himself as worldly-wise is married to one woman but captivated by a much more bohemian and exotic countess. The man and the countess are riding in a carriage, and she responds to his intimations. She asks, "Is it your idea, then, that I should live with you as your mistress—since I can't be your wife?"

The man's response is from 100 years ago, but it is timeless. "I want–I want somehow to get away with you into a world where words like that—categories like that—won't exist. Where we shall simply be two human beings who love each other, who are the whole life to each other; and nothing else on earth will matter."

The countess, however, has had too much experience. She responds, "Oh, my dear—where is that country? Have you ever been there? . . . I know so many who've tried to find it, and, believe me, . . . it wasn't at all different from the old world they'd left, but only rather smaller and dingier and more promiscuous."

Here is a truth we try so hard to ignore. Our sexual freedom, in the end, doesn't bring us to the open world we thought it would. Instead, we end up in a world that is just a little smaller and dingier and a bit more promiscuous.

The Consecrated Virgin

I like to watch the process of how ideas permeate a culture. Just a little more than 100 years ago, the psychoanalyst Sigmund Freud was writing about his understanding of the human being and how important our sexual desires are in determining who we are. People felt the freedom of a truth when they took his ideas and understood much of our behavior in terms of sexual desires. In a way, sexuality was interpreted as the determiner of who we were.

These ideas percolated through the intellectuals and artists in the 1920s and 1930s in Europe. By the time I was in college in the 1970s, the ideas were the rage, even in small colleges outside the major cities. Now we see these same ideas in people at large. And if sexuality is the determiner of who we are, any attempt to put boundaries on those freedoms will be understood as oppression.

From the Christian viewpoint, sexuality is powerful, and magnificent, but it has been understood as the handmaid of who we are, not the king. Our sexual penchant is not the core of our person. This fact does not deny the power of sexuality in proper or improper forms. Augustine was a brilliant man and loved the ladies. He had a child out of wedlock. When God began to work on him, he is famously said to have said, "Lord, make me pure . . . but not yet." We can see how much things have changed in our own time. Most attempts to hold up chastity as a virtue would be considered as a reason for humor in our current media. We could hardly say the word *chastity* with a straight face.

Sister Wendy on public television is someone who does not fit into our current conceptions of freedom. She is a "consecrated virgin" in her order, and is only allowed to spend two hours a day at her work. The rest of her time is in prayer. When she does a show on paintings, she seems to shock people. They expect a nun to be like the caricature of a nun on a corny sitcom. Instead, shs seems like the most free and joyful person on TV. She seems very liberated, in an upside-down sort of way. It makes one think.

It's funny how strong our preconceptions are, and how much they shape the way we see things. For much of college, I didn't believe in God. I was confident that all of this experience came about by time plus space plus chance. In one of my classes, we were studying the irrational, and we had to read about the ecstatic experiences of Theresa of Avila. The next day in class, I felt smarter than the other more respectful students. "She's nothing but a sexually frustrated, middle-aged woman," I remember saying. I was so sure. I had read Freud. But intellectually, there is great danger when someone says "nothing but." How can we know for sure as we so confidently exclude someone's experience with God? Now that I believe in God, I am much more respectful. I am much more careful before I classify someone according to their sexual proclivities.

Wendy Shalit wrote a wonderful book called *A Return to Modesty*. In it, she puzzled about the categories we use in terms of sexuality. She wasn't a Christian and didn't seem to me to have an axe to grind. She noticed at college that the girls who proclaimed and acted out the most that they had no sexual hindrances really didn't seem free at all. They were often ones who were acting out their hurts through cutting their wrists or some other behavior such as bulimia. On the other hand, the ones who seemed to have the most restrictions concerning sexual activity, the women of the Hasidic Jewish context at the school, seemed the happiest and most free. She puzzled at this paradox.

How we treat sexuality and the commitments involved will have deep implications for our society. One of my sons works as a lawyer in Brooklyn. He grew up since the age of two months old in the Lower East Side in Manhattan. He worked with many of our kids in the neighborhood, and reflected on the broken parts of their lives. Thinking of all the problems here — homelessness, drug dealing, gangs, unemployment, and illiteracy — he came up with the following question: What would help this neighborhood more than anything else?

His answer surprised me. He said the thing that would help the most would be if the father of the child in this neighborhood truly loved the mother. I think he is right, at least for here. What if each man was a promise keeper, and married the woman, and stuck with her for life? This would have more impact on our city than just about anything. So many of the men in this neighborhood are absent, or with other women, or staying somewhere else. What would happen if there was a loving, committed father in every household? I think the change in the metropolis would be incalculable.

We work with a group of men in our mission who seek to be promise keepers. As the men began to trust each other, and delve into their own past and their own families, we found that most of them had absent fathers, and a few of them had fathers that were a distant part of their lives. Let's be honest. This reality is partly a result of how we look at sexuality.

Chaos theory has become a part of our vocabulary. It has helped us understand the fact that small changes can have large, unexpected consequences. A butterfly wing moving in one place can eventually shape the direction of a hurricane. The person who invented the combustion engine probably didn't think about the possibility that his invention would eventually destroy the noble Sequoia trees in the Sierra Nevada through car pollution. We often can't anticipate what the later results will be of our choices. We will see some consequences, some perhaps for good, but some perhaps for ill in the promotion of a different sexual ethic. We are considering rights, and one of the rights of a child is to know who the father and mother is. We are already beginning to reap heartache in the sperm donor industry, as children look to identify their biological fathers. Whatever actions we take now will no doubt have long-term implications for generations down the line.

It's probably safe to say that we have no idea what consequences will come from our different sexual codes and treatment of commitment in marriage. I remember listening to a speaker at New York University in a discussion of sexual ethics. He mused a bit on the idea of unintended consequences. He said the Egyptian royalty 3,000 years ago thought it was a great idea to have a biological brother marry his sister and ensure the containment of the royal line. They may have even scoffed at more reactionary groups like the Hebrews who prohibited it. It would be another 3,000 years, when scientist Gregor Mendel's work on genetics would begin to explain a bit of the consequences of their actions, that we began to understand the prohibition a bit more. So often we may not know the consequences of our actions for generations. Again, what seemed like freedom in the Egyptian royalty, turned out to be a different and far worse kind of bondage.

When we deal with things that affect our own desires and the lives of our children's children so deeply, it seems important to me to take care as we proceed. To be honest,

I see people every day who are dealing with the trauma and lack of security in their own lives, because of the so-called sexually free choices their parents made. We need to be careful with each other, because the issues in sexuality are so tender. But before we pull down a wall, it is always important to remember why it was put up.

No doubt our desires will affect how we see things. Even an intellectual with the integrity of English writer Aldous Huxley admitted that his philosophy as a young man was mostly based on his desire to be free from a certain kind of sexual morality. At least he was honest. We all have to deal with the insight that we see what we want to see, and we choose the way with mixed motives.

I have quoted before Mencius: "In order to decide what we are to do, we first must decide what we will not do." So many walls have been torn down by our culture, we may need to work toward freedom by building walls. We need to set boundaries on our evaluation of life using money. We need to set boundaries on what is accepted in married life. As quoted at the beginning of *The Lord of the Rings*, the innkeeper, Mr. Butterbur, didn't much like the rangers, who roamed the countryside. But in the end, once they were gone, many enemies began to invade his home. He said he didn't know what those rangers did until they were gone. In the same way, we may not realize what the walls did until they are gone. Desire for money and desire for romantic fulfillment need to have boundaries, or they become idolatry. And in the long run, idolatry just doesn't work.

principle #6
Limit Your Actions — The Prison of Busyness

You and the people with you will certainly wear yourselves out, for the thing is too heavy for you. You are not able to do it alone."

EXODUS 18:18

"When we live without listening to the timing of things, when we live and work in twenty-four-hour shifts without rest — we are on war time, mobilized for battle. Yes, we are strong and capable people, we can work without stopping, faster and faster, electric lights making artificial day so the whole machine can labor without ceasing. But remember: No living thing lives like this. There are greater rhythms, seasons and hormonal cycles and sunsets and moonrises and great movements of seas and stars. We are part of the creation story, subject to all its laws and rhythms."

— *Wayne Muller,* Sabbath: Finding Rest, Renewal, *and* Delight in Our Busy Lives

Scandalous, Particular Love

I talk about this concept of limiting our actions all the time, but the paradox is hard to capture in words. Recently, I stopped doing what I normally do for a while. I got away from work. I sat outside at a table in the sun one morning. I had choices in what I could think about. I knew I had about 270 emails, people who wanted and needed my attention. In those emails were a bunch of "understood" commitments on my part. I knew I needed to look at them to fulfill all the commitments that make up who I am. I could have spent the morning thinking about them and working on them.

But instead, I chose that morning to do something else. I chose to take the time to write a letter, using pen and paper. I had not written a letter like that, with pen and paper, for a long time. It was a bigger endeavor in terms of time commitment. It took me all morning to write the letter as I sat in the sun. In a sense, I had wasted a lot of time that could have been used more efficiently to do the email work that was a part of my profession.

Yet here is the paradox. I felt so fulfilled, and in a deeper sense, well, efficient. I wrote to a man whom I cared about. I knew I should have done it a long time ago. I took time. I thought about him. I thought about what I was writing. He was in jail, and I knew he would take the time to read the letter carefully. How could I have been more "efficient" by going at this snail's pace rather than responding to 270 requests in the same morning?

I finished the morning feeling right. I saw more clearly the nature of love. There were countless things I could have done that morning. There were countless things I wanted to do. There were countless things other people wanted me to do. But I limited myself to one person, one slow method, one time.

Love is always doing this. A mother could be doing many other practical and even loving things, but she refuses to do those things so she can focus on that one child, her own son or daughter, that one time. A friend clears the calendar for all the necessary things he or she should be doing, for that one friend and that one evening. Even God in the Bible limits all the things He could be manifesting all the time so that we can hear the manifestation to that one person, Abraham. The fact that God chooses to speak at that one time, with that one event, is part of what some theologians call "the scandal of particularity."

Sometimes in our desire to please everyone and do everything, we forget the freedom of being scandalous in that way. Even though we could be using all our time and resources for the poor, or some other good cause, instead, we lavish our resources and our heart on that one person. This is one way to define love. It is saying, "I am not doing many things, in order to do this one thing for you."

Looking at the world this way helps us understand the woman who poured a very expensive ointment on the head of Jesus. The disciples were indignant because the funds from this one ointment could have been used to help many others. Jesus understood this lavishing of care at one place and one time (Matthew 26:6–13). Of course Mary showed a kind of love too, choosing the *"one thing that was necessary,"* when there were so many obligations and expectations society said should could and should be fulfilling (Luke 10:41–42).

The Time Prison

The busier we get, the less we think about this paradox. Often, by doing less than we planned, we do more. When we attempt to do more and more, we get caught in a prison, no matter how "good" our original intentions are. It is a prison of busyness. We see these prisoners everywhere, good people, who because of their goodness, have taken on so much that the joy of life has been drained from them. Their life was originally like a bright watercolor. Their life, however, has been caught in a storm of responsibilities, and the vivid colors have all been washed away. All that is left is a streaked etching of what their life could have been.

Busyness is a trap that often conceals a core problem underneath a patina of good intentions. The next sentence might hurt, but I have to say it to myself often. No matter how much "good" we are doing, the core problem is an issue of pride and control. We feel that without us, the right things won't be done. We must work even harder if we are going to control the outcome. When problems arise, it is all up to us, so we work even harder still. In the end, we find that we cannot control what is happening, but we feel caught in a web of commitments. Before we know it, we are resenting the people around us. Why am I working late and getting up early, while they seem to be just hanging out and having a blast? Worst of all, we are becoming more and more self-righteous, and we are not even aware of the prison we are building around ourselves.

In another time and environment, Isaiah gives us a read on how destructive busyness and rushing can be. Chapter 30 is one of the most amazing chapters to me in the whole Bible. The people of God see impending disaster, and they rush around to make plans and alliances. Unfortunately, the plan is not God's plan. *"'Ah, stubborn children,' declares the Lord, 'who carry out a plan, but not mine, and who make an alliance, but not of my Spirit, that they may add sin to sin'"* (30:1).

As the chapter proceeds, God essentially tells them to calm down and be quiet. *"'In returning and rest you shall be saved; in quietness and in trust shall be your strength'"* (30:15).

The people, however, decide that frenetic activity is a better way to go. In the same verse, God points out what they did. *"'But you were unwilling, and you said, 'No! We will flee upon horses'; therefore you shall flee away; and 'We will ride upon swift steeds'; therefore your pursuers shall be swift"* (30:15–16). Ironically, the very attempt to use speed for efficiency precipitates their destruction. Like a mouse, the faster it scurries away, the faster it triggers the pounce reflex from the cat. We may not understand the entire context that Isaiah was addressing, but we all know the feeling of choosing our own plan to resolve a situation, and finding that our very attempt to work things out complicated the problem even more.

Sadly, hurry is the disease of our time. In an earlier book on leadership, I wrote a chapter, "Don't Just Do Something, Stand There." It discussed our tendency as leaders to rush in and "resolve" a problem without listening to God. I also talked about the discipline of taking a Sabbath, a day to not work, to remember that we are the created and not the Creator. I will not repeat what I have already written.

Yet here is the image of the time prison. You see it in the student at school who never enjoys himself even on weekends because of all the things he should be doing. You see it in the bride preparing for her own huge wedding. You see it in the investor at Wall Street who cannot enjoy his own family because of the extra hours he is required to work. Busyness is invasive and tends to try to poison everything.

Before we realize it, this prison brings us into deeper and deeper entrapment. Sooner or later, we find ourselves in the prison of exhaustion. It is very hard for the Holy Spirit to do a fresh and creative thing in us when we are totally exhausted.

Sound and Speed

*B*eing confused by our own activity and seeking diversion instead of true rest, we enter the prison of constant sound. We find that we must always have on our earphones, or we must watch TV, or we must have the news blaring, or we must have the radio talk show on. This meaningless entertainment is a substitute for real rest. Our society encourages this kind of diversion instead of true rest by making sound always available. Even if the Holy Spirit were speaking to us, we could not hear it, because of the chatter of advertisements for deodorant or for antacids. Huxley said that a society is good to the extent that it renders contemplation possible for its members. If this were the criteria, our society would be judged the most barbaric. In my own travels, I am fascinated to watch that even families that take the time and expense to go to some beautiful place to go camping, will often bring out a big boom box and fill the air with its noise, neutralizing the rustle of leaves and the sound of the birds around them.

When the writer Aleksandr Solzhenitsyn was released from the Soviet Union, he eventually came to the United States. He knew a thing or two about imprisonment, spending many years in a Soviet work camp. What he observed, as he looked at the faces of the people in the West, was sadness, despite the political freedoms they had. In his famous speech in 1978 at

Harvard, he made a telling comment. It is granted that he had been the subject of many human rights abuses in the Soviet Union. However, the West needed help too. They needed to have the right not to be barraged by an excessive flow of trivial and meaningless information—"gossip, nonsense, vain talk." "Hastiness and superficiality," he said, was a part of the "psychic disease" of our time.

The inflow of this meaningless information is so common, that we don't even think of it as confining. We are in a prison of unawareness. We don't even think how banal the constant advertisements about drugs for asthma, kitchen cleaners, shampoos, and fast cars are upon our soul. We sing mindless fast food songs as if they were Bach. We have become unaware of the pettiness of the reality shows and the comedies, where two-thirds of the jokes refer to either sexual innuendo or potty humor. If anyone objects, they are accused of being a prig. This endless flow of banality is like a quicksand, and we are asleep as we slowly sink below the surface.

Assisting the prison of constant chatter is the confinement of speed. We move more and more quickly in order to evade we don't know what. Like rocking in a rocking chair, we move and create the illusion that we are making progress.

Many years ago, Milan Kundera wrote a novel called *Slowness*. I didn't think the novel was very good, but I love the title. Kundera reflected on how we treat our life. He said that whenever we want to forget something, we will naturally walk more and more quickly. But if we wish to remember something, we will walk more and more slowly. His point could relate to our society. It seems to be moving faster and faster. What are we trying to forget? On the other hand, part of the role of Christ in the gospel is to help us remember our song when we have forgotten it. He came to the busy and preoccupied Matthew, dealing with 100 lucrative tax issues, looked him in the eyes, and asked him to leave it all in order to follow (Matthew 9:9). I think that in some way, he reminded Matthew of the faint echo of who he really was. Memory returned.

I wouldn't agree with Carl Jung, the psychiatrist, about a number of things. However, he made this comment about our times. He said that hurry was not of the devil, it was the devil. Even non-Christians understand the satanic nature of hurry.

In *The Chronicles of Narnia*, the Lion says that no one is ever told what would have happened. However, in the first three chapters of the Bible, one wonders if God was going to allow the couple to eat of the tree of knowledge of good and evil at the appropriate time. We, however, couldn't wait. Even though there was a seemingly endless yes and only one no in the whole garden, we still were convinced we needed to take a short cut to get the goodies. In some ways, all sin is like that. We are in a hurry, and we can't wait. We've decided to take a short cut to the things that are good. And as we all know, paradoxically, shortcuts make long delays.

The sad thing is, that once we get on one of those long delays and see that we are losing more time, our personal tendency is to go faster and faster. There we are, scurrying in a frenzy along the path, and it is the wrong path. The worst part of all is that we have convinced ourselves that rushing is the right thing to do, even though we vaguely know that something is wrong.

Saying the Holy No

We have already mentioned a royal road to freedom. The Chinese philosopher Mencius, thousands of years ago, put it quite simply. He said that we must decide what we are not to do. Then we can freely do what we are called to do. Once again, the freedom comes in limitation. We make the choice not to rush.

This attitude usually involves stopping in some way. Hopefully, people see that they must get off the merry-go-round on their own. Hopefully it doesn't take a time in the hospital or in jail or in some other desperate situation, where clearly a person really has no other active resources. Oddly enough, in our work in New York, I have seen how jail or some other confinement has been the path to freedom. Go figure.

The Bible says it quite clearly in David's book of songs. *"Be still, and know that I am God"* (Psalm 46:10). If we don't stop and realize that all our concerns are not the hub, but part of the spokes of a vast universe beyond our little comprehension, it is hard to break away from the chains of busyness. It is hard to know even where to begin.

At our mission, we are blessed to have many people who are hard workers, who are pouring their lives out to help those who have fallen through the cracks. But the prison of busyness is insidious and can get any of us. One of my co-workers keeps me accountable, and I work to keep him accountable. One time I gave him a coin to carry in his pocket. On one side, the coin simply says, *Yes*. On the other side, it says, *No*. It is a reminder of something we say over and over. Before you can say the *holy yes*, you must be able to say the *holy no*. How sad if someone who loves God and seeks to invite the poor, the maimed, the lame, and the blind, then becomes himself or herself a frenzied chicken with its head cut off, rushing around, running into everyone, seeking to help, spreading the anxiety.

The way out of this prison then is not to work harder, even if the things you are working on are good. The way out of this prison is paradoxically to limit your activities. It means setting boundaries. You and I cannot do everything for everyone. In the excellent book *Having a Mary Heart in a Martha World* by Joanna Weaver, a story is told about a man who is given by God a few stones to carry to the top of the hill. As he proceeds, a number of people along the way each ask for a little bit of help carrying their loads. Eventually, carrying the load up the hill becomes almost unbearable, and the man in resentment complains to God for His unfairness in requiring him to do such an impossible task. God, in effect, responds that He never told the man to take all those other loads. God takes them out, and the man's load becomes easy again.

This story obviously does not mean that we are to close our eyes to those in need, but it does mean we are to listen to what God has for us to do. We cannot do everything for everyone.

Even the earthly Jesus did not seem to do that. He did not do everything that everyone wanted Him to do when they wanted Him to do it, and neither can we. When Lazarus was ill, Jesus stayed where He was two more days. The Bible says that He was at least four days late in arriving to heal Lazarus. When Jesus arrived, Martha quickly let Him know that if He had come sooner, Lazarus would be alive (John 11:21).

It seems as though at least some of the people there have a better idea about what Jesus should have done.

We have to remind ourselves of this fact. We do not have enough time to do all the things that other people think we should do. But we do have enough time to do what God wants us to do. Once we limit our action to what God has for us, regardless of our own frenzied, personal script, or the constant expectations of others, we become free once again.

Recently a group of young pastors asked me how we are to manage time to ourselves in our present day. The pressures and requirements from others are so great, what with email, texting, Twitter, Facebook, etc. The world has simply made things too busy. I reminded them that throughout history people have been plagued with the demands of busyness. These demands didn't arrive in our generation. Marcus Aurelius in the second century talks about all the demands on his time too. To be honest, I imagine the pressures were far greater on him than on us. He says, however, a very important thing. He says don't talk about the fact that you have no leisure. Don't be one of those people who is always saying how busy they are. They are always mentioning how little time they have.

Marcus Aurelius has a point. We build a reality with our words. If we are constantly talking about how busy we are, we deprive ourselves of the joy in the time we do have. The Bible says that death and life are in the power of the tongue (Proverbs 18:21). We are to take care that we do not build a reality with our words.

God gives us a kind of manual for freedom in Exodus. Here the people of God have lived as slaves for a long time. Even after they get out of bondage, they must relearn how they talk, act, and view things. Moses, on the other hand, grew up in a palace, and should be able to think as a prince. However, he succumbs to the prison of busyness, just as so many others have before him and after him. His responsibilities begin to enslave him.

His own father-in-law is the one who is able to tell him the truth. He sees Moses toiling from morning to night, adjudicating all the tough decisions for the people of God as they move to this new phase. It seems like the right thing to do; He is doing the best he can. Can you blame Moses? But Jethro comes to him and tells him straight. *"What you are doing is not good. You and the people will certainly wear yourselves out, for the thing is too heavy for you. You are not able to do it alone"* (Exodus 18:17–18).

Jethro's advice is helpful. Get other people to help. Often we are not quite as important as we think we are. This may be true in running a nation, but also in working at a job or running a family. The woman with two young children may need to think of the same principle. Can the children be given some responsibility? It is better for them. They will learn something and be more involved. It is better at work. When I was a teacher in graduate school, I learned quickly that things go better if I stopped trying to juggle all the mechanics of running a class, and assigned each student a responsibility. Graduate school can be boring enough if all you do is sit and take notes.

Here is a good discipline that I am working on. When you make the list of things you have to do each day, can you involve or deputize someone else to help you do some of them? By trying to do too much, you may be depriving someone of what God wants them to do, and they may be able eventually to do the job much better than you. This is part of Jethro's advice in Exodus 18. Get good people to help you so that it won't be such a burden for you. I am slowly learning that by trying to do everything myself, I am not being humble. Instead, I am sometimes depriving someone else of the thing that they could do. So I have a new mode of self-talk. Instead of increasing your actions, limit your actions. Make a list of all the things each day you will not do. It is an inverted path to freedom.

principle #7

Give When You Are Empty—The Prison of Selfishness

"Tell all the congregation of Israel that in the tenth day of this month every man shall take a lamb according to their fathers' houses, a lamb for a household."

EXODUS 12:3

"I'm sorry, boy . . . but I have nothing left to give you."

—The Giving Tree

The Giving Beggar

It was my first time in the Lower East Side a long time ago. I had no idea that I would be spending my life there. I was a young man. As we walked down the avenue, I saw men who were drunk lying against the buildings. One man had defecated in his pants. His pants had been pulled down, and there were flies everywhere around him as he slept. The park seemed filthy too, filled with dog manure and old vomit.

A crumpled man probably noticed that we were new and asked us for money. We already knew enough not to give him money, not to participate further in the problems of his life. We offered, however, to buy him a slice of pizza. He seemed delighted. He said he was very hungry. We ordered the pizza and spent some time talking to him. He was cordial and not at all what I had feared.

Once he got the pizza, he turned to us and asked politely. "Do you mind if I take this slice to my buddy Joe? He is really hungry, and he needs it even more than me. He held the hot pizza as if it were a treasure and walked away, I presume to find Joe. I never saw him again.

I never knew this man's story, and the older, cynical me wonders what kind of scam he might have been after. However, I like to think that this man, in the middle of his own addiction and need, was thinking beyond himself, thinking about his buddy. I remember saying to my friend that if I were hungry and desperate, I certainly wouldn't be thinking about some other guy named Joe. I would have scarfed up that pizza and then planned what I would do for Joe afterward.

Since that time, I have seen this path to freedom so many times. People who seem extremely needy will find a way to help someone else. The brutally abused woman will find a way to provide clothes for others. The man who has been sent to jail will find a way to bless a family. The beggar on the street gives his last dollar bill away. It goes on and on. For me, when I see this kind of attitude, I think that it is often a sign of health.

I am continually astonished to see people who seem to be absolutely empty, to have nothing, who reach out and give to others. It sometimes becomes their road to freedom.

Let me put it this way. The ones who get whole serve others. My friends in Alcoholics Anonymous know this as a survival technique. The recovering alcoholic has got to think beyond himself and help other alcoholics, or he will lose in his own recovery.

Once, I was on the campus at my son's college, and I saw this quote on a plaque there. It was by Albert Schweitzer, an academic who eventually gave his life to medical missions in the Congo. This is what he said:

> "The only ones among you who will be really happy are those who will have sought and found how to serve."

We know this truth deep in our spirits, and we find it in the gospels. Jesus describes this flow of life, which I have seen so often as people move toward freedom: *"Give, and it shall be given to you. Good measure, pressed down, shaken together, running over, will be put into your lap. For with the measure you use it will be measure back to you"* (Luke 6:38).

In dealing with people, my wife has often told a story which she remembers seeing in a movie as a small child. She thinks it is a Disney movie, but realizes it may be a conflation of a lot of memories. In her memory, there is a crippled child who has found a way to use his sickness as a means of manipulating the people around him. He is self-centered and his life is very narrow. The one thing he cares about is his pet bird in a cage. One day, the bird had gotten loose. To the little boy's horror, he saw the family cat moving closer and closer to pounce on his bird. Before he knew it, he was standing up out of his wheelchair. He was passionately thinking about something besides himself. It became the way to health.

As my wife counsels others, she will often help them think about something other than themselves. We both feel that it is a path to freedom. At our church and community center, people will often quote Isaiah 58 when people are caught in the gloom of their own dire circumstances. Verse 10 says, *"If you pour yourself out for the hungy, and satisfy the desire of the afflicted, then shall your light rise in the darkness and your gloom be as the noonday."* This truth is a secret many know but we forget when we are caught in the gloom of life's difficulties. Somehow, helping others becomes an antidote for our own self-pity. Our gloom becomes something else.

We might as well say it in a way that is blunt. People who are selfish don't heal. To me, their selfishness places them at the center of things, and that situation does not reflect reality. Once they see that they are connected to everything else, they are more in a position to receive true healing, not just a temporary cure that money might buy. Giving to others protects us from the prison of selfishness.

The Prison Gardener

Nelson Mandela is a man to watch. Many years ago, when apartheid gripped South Africa, the mission I was helping in Harlem hosted South Africans who had come secretly to speak about the horrible things there. Their own government said that what they did was illegal. We talked into the night about what might happen. At that time, most of these people, fighting for freedom, felt as though some kind of bloodbath was inevitable. Given the horrible oppression, how could it be otherwise?

Mandela, one of the primary leaders of the anti-apartheid movement there, was placed in prison for 27 years. His remarkable autobiography, *Long Walk to Freedom*, tells part of the story. As I read the story, because I live in such a different context, I wondered how Mandela continued. How did he keep from being bitter, as he watched his most productive years being drained away in prison? How could he stand these people imprisoning him, people who felt that he did not have a right to even vote because of the color of his skin?

His journey is a remarkable one and worth thinking about. For me, as I read his story, I saw one incident as a parable of what Mandela had to do to lead his people to freedom. For a long time, he did hard labor in a lime quarry, and was allowed only one visitor and one letter every six months. Often the letter was mangled by censors. As the years went by, he was allowed to tend a garden. He used it to grow vegetables. He gave the vegetables to the other inmates. Remarkably, he also gave vegetables to the guards for their family. A prisoner has such limited choices, but he took steps within the choices he had. "The garden was one of the few things in prison that one could control," he said. This action of gardening was in some ways a metaphor for what the people of South Africa would have to do. Mandela gave food to his oppressors as well as his fellow inmates. By taking steps for good in such an environment, he made an upside-down statement on freedom. He served the very people who were trying to keep his mind in a cage. He himself made the choice to do so. He refused the prison of bitterness, and gave when he had practically nothing. Eventually, he was set free.

The account of his influence on helping South Africa move to a new stage without the kind of expected violence is one of the great stories of our time. For me, he started that story in prison when he had nothing and every reason to take a different path.

God shows the power of giving as people were deeply oppressed in the Bible. When the people of God are caught in slavery in Egypt, they apparently have very little. They are slaves. It fascinates me that one of the first things God asks them to do is to give something, to offer something. He says that each family should offer up a lamb (Exodus 12:3). Why should they do that? They have so little. They are slaves. Shouldn't they keep that lamb for their own time of need as they face survival in the desert? Isn't it time for God to give something to them, since they are so enslaved? But I think that there is deep psychological understanding in the instructions. God is going to help them stop thinking like slaves, like victims. The path to being released from Egypt asks for each of them to offer up something that in their situation would have been very valuable. It's the inside job that is important. God could have done it a different way.

This inner journey from moving from a slave mentality to the mentality of a free person continues. Once the people are set free from Egypt, one of the first things that God asks them to do is offer up the beautiful things they have in order to make something beautiful for God—a tabernacle. It seems as though He asks them to form a kind of arts committee. Making something beautiful inevitably makes you think beyond yourself and your own problems.

I have watched this with men in prison. They may act tough on the streets, but when they are in prison, some choose to make beautiful drawings or tapestries for the church or for other people. We have one of the tapestries hanging on our wall in church. This giving of beauty is a path to inner freedom because it brings them beyond themselves, and they can give even when they have so little. We all know this is true. It is so sad when the more we accumulate, the less we remember this path.

Jesus gives us an example of a person who is hurting and chooses to serve. In the Book of John, Jesus knows He is about to die and that He is going to be betrayed by one of His own. This realization must have been crushing to Him. Yet, we find that in that most devastating of circumstances, He takes a towel and washes the disciples' feet. He gives from the deepest sorrow. It is an inverse way to freedom.

The Hands of a Bag Lady

A long time ago, a college student was working at our mission and was helping a bag lady. He had done a lot of things for her so that she could survive, and one day, she put some cash in his hand. He didn't want to embarrass her, and he asked me what he should do with it. I told him to keep it. It was not so important for him to have it, but it was important for her to give it.

Recently, I had a discussion with a person about ultimate things. This person had some very different premises than I did. He made this comment, "In a trillion years, none of these truths will matter."

That comment got me thinking. A trillion years is a long time. We don't quite know how to imagine that kind of time. Some current scientific thought thinks our universe is about 14 billion years old. If the universe began to contract at some point, maybe the universe would survive for 30 or 40 billion years. If another universe was formed, it might also expand and contract in 40 billion years. But 1 trillion is 1,000 billion. Thus, using my friend's projections and assumptions, in 1 trillion years, we might have gone through the lives of 20 universes or more.

We have no sure idea how big a universe is, really, or if there is intelligent life in some form somewhere else. Less than 100 years ago, we thought that this galaxy was all there was. Now we know that there are millions of galaxies. What if there were just one form of intelligent "life" in each universe, or what if there were two or three? What would be a truth that would still be true in 1 trillion years?

I think what Jesus did as He washed the betrayer's feet is that truth—that self-sacrificing love. Even if there was some kind of other life, and even if many of those "intelligences" chose other ways, such as brute force, even if they acted like a Nazi society, or in *Star Trek* terms, like Klingons, that same truth would still be true. *"God so loved the world, that he gave his only Son"* (John 3:16). Because this way is the truth, there is freeing power in it.

In Psalm 16:11, David understands that God is one who will not leave us alone. "You make known to me the path of life." This self-giving love is the path of life. It always will be.

principle #8

Be Really Stubborn—The Prison of Discouragement

"The Lord will fulfill his purpose for me; your steadfast love, O Lord, endures forever."

PSALM 138:8

"Self-pity is our worst enemy, and if we yield to it, we can never do anything wise in this world."

—Helen Keller

Small and Shy

She was hardly five feet tall. During her years as a high school teacher for girls, one co-worker described her as "very small, quiet, and shy." Another member of her group described her as "ordinary." Yet on a train, she felt a call to help the poor. In the next few years, she had to surmount many technicalities of the church bureaucracy to be released from her job in order to work on the streets. She had to find a place to live and a way to get on, being used to having many of the necessities provided for her in her past life. As she worked with the poorest, and took a stand for their rights, people began to notice some qualities that were not so "ordinary."

One of those qualities was persistence. One might even call her stubborn as she refused to buckle to the expectations of others in treating those who didn't seem to matter too much. One expects freedom to come from lack of restrictions and wealth, yet she eventually stood up to world leaders and showed a kind of freedom in the midst of severe self-discipline and poverty. In those early days on the streets, her name was Teresa. Eventually she was known as Mother Teresa. Even as an old woman, frail and bent, she refused to stop.

We sometimes think of the sweet, kind person that came to the United States and shared about widening the circle of compassion. She was all about kindness, right? We forget her address to our nation about the rights of the unborn. We forget her stubbornness in the inner city streets of her adopted home.

Occasionally we think of the "free spirit" as the one who is flexible, yielding in circumstances, tolerant, a kind of go-with-the-flow sort of person. Well, in some circumstances, that kind of attitude may be true. However, clearly in the important things, there is a tenacity, a stubbornness, in a freedom fighter. Without it, we learn that eventually not much freedom happens.

When God begins to work in a person, and begins to release that person from some addiction, or some idolatry that has gripped them for a long time, we know that there will be some needed stubbornness. Because usually, there will be some serious resistance to the surge toward freedom.

As the people of God learned in Egypt, there will be a Pharaoh, there will be a top-notch military army, there will be thirst, there will be hunger, there will be setbacks, there will be giants. Some obstacle always seems to crop up. That resistance is just part of the freedom process. Without it, we don't grow and become the free person we were meant to be. Flabbiness is not part of the birthright of the free. As we encounter challenging circumstances on the outside, we grow on the inside. And we know by now that the freedom is really an inside job.

It is hard to estimate the power of the person who says, "I am not quitting." Once a person realizes the heart of God and God's desire for good and freedom despite the present circumstances, that determination rises up and often even assists in clearing the way. There was a saying where I grew up, and it contains a spiritual truth: if you are willing to stand forever, it won't take very long.

Faith issues are all about patience and persistence. I heard a man tell me when I first became a Christian that the greatest sin against faith is to quit. Even if we mess up, even if we do something wrong, God can still work with us and make adjustments if we do not quit. But when we quit, it is very hard for Him to do something with us, because God is such a freedom fighter in the deepest sense. He will not violate our freedom. A second-century Christian made this statement: "Compulsion is no attribute of God." God will not force us. Therefore, if we quit, we limit what God can do with us.

I love the King James translation of Psalm 78:41: "Yea, they turned back and tempted God, and limited the Holy One of Israel." By turning back, it sounds as though in one sense they limited what God was willing to do to bless them and bring them freedom.

Washington and Churchill

Of course, we see a kind of stubbornness in freedom fighters in our world all the time.

I live close to the East River in New York City. I can walk along it and muse on the fog that saved George Washington's army. Without the fog, the Revolution might have been snuffed out right in New York. As Washington retreated, there was time after time when the army could have been completely destroyed. Looking back, Washington called their survival, "almost a miracle."

Part of that survival was Washington's persistence. He fought the Revolution for eight years and only went home one time during those years. He understood what so many of us seeking to break free of a personal bondage forget: "To survive is to succeed." Washington lost battles, but he refused to allow those losses to crush him or the army. In some ways, our nation got its freedom because of his bulldog tenacity.

We can't forget another bulldog, one who refused to give up in fighting for the freedom of the Western world in World War II. When Winston Churchill came to visit Harrow School, he wanted to make sure that even the words of the song they sang reflected that tenacity. The song used the phrase, "darker times." He asked that the phrase be changed to "sterner times." He felt that even the words we used were important in avoiding getting into the dumps about our difficulties. He didn't want people to get caught up in a cycle of discouragement. He said that these were our greatest times. "These are not dark days; these are great days—the greatest days our country has ever lived." In his speech to the boys at the school, he summarized the stubbornness that is important if we are to have freedom. "Never give in. Never give in. Never, never, never, never—in nothing, great or small, large or petty—never give in, except to convictions of honor and good sense." That attitude is the road to freedom.

I remember reading what Churchill's favorite Bible verse was. It didn't surprise me. It comes from Psalm 112:8 (KJV). *"He shall not be afraid of evil tidings: His heart is fixed, trusting in the Lord. His heart is established, he is not afraid, until he sees his desire upon his enemies."*

The fact that persistence is important in most great endeavors is obvious. Why belabor the point? Because I see that when circumstances threaten to put us in bondage on a personal level, we often give up before the fight has begun. In my work, sometimes I see it on the most obvious level, and it breaks my heart. I see people who have suffered a series of defeats, who may be homeless, sitting at a table in our church. Their head is down, their shoulders are stooped; they cannot look anyone in the eye. Their circumstances, their experience, and often the script they have learned in life tells them nothing will ever get better. They are defeated, and their actions and approach invite more defeat every day. They have stopped believing anything can go better for them.

This person displays clearly the defeat we experience when we give up. But I see the same streak of defeat in people who will never be homeless. They have given up on the joy of life, on relationships, on value. They often have a tired look. Some wear an expression of cynicism that tells you that surely nothing will ever change. Once again, their approach to life draws the very results they are anticipating.

An expert on trauma was once teaching our staff how to deal with crises like 9/11. He was a professional counselor for terminally ill cancer patients, and I know he did not make statements lightly. Yet he said this, "There is a hidden arrogance in despair. Despair presumes to know that nothing good can ever come out of the present circumstances." Certainly this statement is hard to hear when one is in the depths of an oppressive situation, whatever it is. But the statement gives one pause to think.

We are touching on a truth that is beneath the superficial, "sunshiney" power of positive thinking literature. Hundreds of self-help books promote this kind of "think positive" philosophy. But when we are thinking of the process of achieving real freedom, there is a truth in a saying we had in the Midwest: "Can't never did nothin'." Once we say that things are hopeless, we are usually right.

The Boxer Who Got Knocked Down the Most

The streets where I work are full of people who have given up hope. This approach, of discouragement and despair, is very hard to escape, because the approach is self-fulfilling. It can see no good. The person following this approach is like the man described in the Book of Jeremiah, a man who *"trusts in man."* He is like a parched shrub in the desert, and he *"shall not see any good come"* (17:6). It sounds as though he cannot see the good come because of his own attitude.

I find that the description of the coming Messiah includes a strong refusal to be discouraged. As the Messiah comes, the ultimate freedom fighter, we learn that He comes as a suffering servant. *"He will not grow faint or be discouraged till he has established justice in the earth"* (Isaiah 42:4). This is a core part of who Jesus is. He refuses to be discouraged. In Luke, he "set his face to go to Jerusalem" and refuses to be dissuaded (Luke 9:51).

This is the quality that the freedom fighter must be prepared for. When we fall, we will rise again. One of the men who have been liberated from drug addiction and rage will often quote a Scripture verse as a marker for his new life of persistence. We both like this one: *"The righteous falls seven times and rises again. But the wicked stumble in times of calamity"* (Proverbs 24:16).

Some of the men in our mission who have been set free from drug addiction are boxing fans. We like to talk about Floyd Patterson, who was knocked down seven times in one round and still won the rematch championship fight. He is said to have stated, "They said I was the fighter who got knocked down the most, but I also got up the most."

Recently, I went to the museum of giant trees in Sequoia National Park. I am so impressed on the East Coast when I find an oak that is several centuries old. Patterson's tenacity reminds me of the trees at Sequoia National Park. Some of the trees are thousands of years old. They've been through fires, floods, storms, devastating winds, yet these trees endured. I noticed that one of the components to their survival was their very thick bark. Sometimes the bark itself was two feet thick. This bark had helped them weather all the storms and fires that came along. I like that fact, because I see that people who survive in the city are ones with a very thick skin or covering—like tree bark. They do not let a temporary storm or fiery setback make them quit. They don't accept discouragement.

Part of stubbornness is the willingness to fight, to refuse to take problems lying down. The story of the liberation of the people of God is a reflection of the importance of the growth in this area. Notice that when the slaves are trapped between the Red Sea and the strongest military machine of the time, Moses tells them this: *"The Lord will fight for you, and you have only to be still"* (Exodus 14:14 RSV). Then God does a mighty act of liberation.

However, once they are free and in the desert, they are attacked by the Amalekites, clearly desert-savvy raiders. Why doesn't God just do some super miraculous thing to deliver His people, as He did in Egypt? No, this time they must fight. These slaves, who have probably not handled weapons for centuries, who have allowed other people to fight for them, are going to have to get weapons and practice and stand up for themselves. As we read the story, God is still in charge of the battle, but this time the people of God have to take part (Exodus 17:8–16). In some way, if we are going to be free, we are going to have to have some fight within us. The direction of that fight has changed, but we still are fighters.

I think David had to deal with discouragement in a powerful way. He had lots of enemies and lots of reasons to be discouraged. He talks to himself when he is discouraged. *"Why are you cast down, O my soul, and why are you in turmoil within me?"* (Psalm 42:5). He talks about being overwhelmed: *"When my heart is overwhelmed, lead me to the rock that is higher than I"* (Psalm 61:2 NKJV). But he is a fighter, and one way or another he talks himself into the hope of the Lord. He refuses to get discouraged. As he needs courage, he reminds himself that the Lord will fulfill his purpose in his life (Psalm 138:8).

David describes himself as a fighter. *"Blessed be the Lord, my rock, who trains my hands for war, and my fingers for battle"* (Psalm 144:1). He will not let any giant cause him to quit, whether it be a horrible family circumstance, or his own personal sin. He is not stopping.

Paul, that constant jailbird, gives us the direction for our own fight. We aren't to fight against flesh and blood. As we have seen, that approach would be like a bull charging the matador's cape and forgetting the matador with his bloody darts. We are to put on the armor to stand against principalities and powers (Ephesians 6:10–20). We are to use things like truth, rightness, the good news of peace, faith, the Word of God. Nobody said we aren't supposed to fight. We are just not supposed to fight people.

In fact, to me, as I read Paul's writings, it seems as though there is only one fight. It is not a fight against circumstances. It is not a fight against people. Paul calls it the fight of faith (1 Timothy 6:12; 2 Timothy 4:7). What is the fight of faith?

Well, to me, it is the fight to believe. I choose to believe that Christ loved me and gave His life for me (Galatians 2:20). I believe that God will use all things for good for those who love Him and are called according to His purpose (Romans 8:28). This will be the fight, to believe that truth despite the present changing situations. This is the fight, to see God's invisible love through the visible circumstances. Once we believe God's love and ultimate plan, then we do not have to fight anything else. We can rest (Hebrews 4:11).

An old saying has helped us not to be in denial about the current situation, but also not to be in denial about the plans for good that God has for us. It goes like this—the facts don't change the truth, but the truth will change the facts. I can state the fact, no matter what it is. I am in bondage. I am in bondage to money, or to drugs, or to gossip, or to other people's opinions, or to a low-paying job, or to an abusive family, or to depression, or to mental illness, or to boredom, or to whatever is keeping us from being free. That may be the fact. But the fact will not change the truth. The truth is that God is a freedom fighter, and He loves you, and He has plans for good for you, and in the end, in ways we cannot even imagine, He can take horrible things, which He hates, and bring good out of them for you. He will find a way, even if it transcends the bounds of time and life as we know it. God has always been that way. Just look at the Cross.

Hudson Taylor is a hero to me. I am so amazed at how God used this man in so many ways. He made a statement that has helped me in many endeavors. The more I think about it, the more kinds of circumstances I think it applies to. He said this about the things that God does: First, it is impossible, then it is difficult, then it is done. When we pray for freedom, sometimes this is the path we see happening. At first, even the idea of freedom seems impossible. But if we will persevere, if we are stubborn in the confidence of what God wants to do, we will probably go through a time, perhaps a long time, when the work to be really free is difficult. Then, as we persist and are faithful, we will one day awake and look back, and we will sigh a sigh of relief. We don't really know how it happened. But it is done.

principle #9
Puncture Your Own Dignity — The Prison of Self-Importance

"And David said to Michal, 'It was before the Lord, who chose me above your father and above all his house, to appoint me as prince over Israel, the people of the Lord — and I will make merry before the Lord.'"

2 SAMUEL 6:21 RSV

"Teach us to care and not to care."

— *T. S. Eliot*

Gallows Humor

I have often reminded a certain kind of person that life is not a game. The things we do matter. There is always a feast of consequences. We are not a zero that can just float through, not thinking about what the results are of our actions. We are given the dignity of having consequences for our actions.

Yet we know in our hearts that along with this deep seriousness, there is a liberating quality in humor, especially humor that includes all of us in the laughter. When things are toughest and seem most confining, some of us have developed the ability to laugh at the situation, while still focusing on the way to freedom.

I suppose that some people call this laughter gallows humor. When things are bleakest and the worst, some people are able to tweak a different perspective on things.

I remember seeing in a store window these words of wisdom, which they claimed came from Italy: "Since the house is on fire, let us warm ourselves." In other words, we are determined to find something good in this situation, no matter how terrible it is.

The earlier English writers loved puns. Sir Walter Raleigh was not only a soldier, he was also a poet. Eventually he was beheaded. In one of his last letters to a friend before his death, he gave a classic example of gallows humor. He wrote, "When

I come to a sad parting [i.e., with his head] you shall see me grave enough." After you groan at such a bad line, it is good to remember that the people of the time saw this as a way to face adversity.

Oscar Wilde the playwright was no stranger to puns. He is said to have made a comment something like this on his deathbed: "Either these curtains go or I do." Whether Wilde said this or not, we get the flavor of this kind of humor used in tough circumstances.

People that have developed this ability have an extra tool in fighting tough circumstances. Those who were alive at the time, all remember Ronald Reagan's line after he was shot in the chest and was being wheeled into emergency surgery. He turned to the chief surgeon, and said, "I hope you are all Republicans."

We see a few examples of a deep laughter in the films. A classic film by John Huston, *The Treasure of the Sierra Madre*, deals with the dark side of human nature. After watching three people recover a large amount of gold we see them increasingly connive and justify their actions as the time when they can cash in on the gold approaches. One of the three shoots the other one, and as he takes the gold, he is killed by some bandits. The bandits think the gold is just sand and scatter it. When the oldest gold miner sees that the gold is all blown away in the wind, with all their labor of ten months brought to nothing, he doesn't scowl or weep. The end of the movie shows him laughing with his friend in the midst of the blowing wind. One supposes he is laughing at all our human folly in our little predicaments of life, in the context of the grander scheme of things. I would call it gallows humor.

I have seen humor used as people found a new life in Christ. One man, who was formerly homeless, talked about the new life of trust he was developing. He just wasn't the type to get too serious on us. He said, "Jesus washed away my sins." Then he looked up. "Sorry about the ring around the bathtub." He continued, "God made us in His image. . . . He must have had the flu when He made me."

Admittedly, these examples are all quite different, but they each accomplish one purpose. They puncture our self-important pomposity.

We know there is a time to fight for our loss of dignity. We also learn there is a time to undercut our own sense of dignity. Humor reminds us that every external thing in this life is going to pass away anyway, so we might as well get a laugh as we go. Proverbs 3:7 encourages us in this truth. It says, "Be not wise in your own eyes." Humor helps us continue to develop ways not to take ourselves so seriously. In one of our Bible studies, where many of the people are in recovery from alcohol or drug addiction, we have a time for our funny friend to give us a one-liner. We call him our "gospel comedian." He is the one who delivered the ring around the bathtub line. Each week he gives us a one-liner so that we can laugh and hopefully not take ourselves so seriously.

The late Zig Ziglar, the motivational speaker, came to our mission church to preach one of the first sermons in our new building. "Don't hold in your laugher," he instructed us. "It will make your thighs spread out."

Pomposity doesn't seem to be the road to freedom. The speaker in Ecclesiastes may be referring to pomposity when he tells us, *"Be not overly righteous, and do not make yourself too wise. Why should you destroy yourself?"* (Ecclesiastes 7:16). In the New Testament, the Pharisees seem to revel in their own self importance. Jesus makes a number of comments and tells several stories that seemed aimed at puncturing their attempts to be righteous over much in the wrong way (e.g., Luke 15:11–32).

Recently one of my best friends from childhood died. He knew he was going to die, and he preached some sermons about not taking life for granted. They were amazing sermons. When I saw him a few weeks before his death, I told him that I thought his most recent sermons were really anointed in a new kind of way. He just shrugged his shoulders and laughed. "Aw, when you are about to die, anything you say sounds deep. You say that life is short, and everyone sighs and says how profound that is. You'll know what I mean one day." He simply refused to take himself too seriously.

The Worst Jokes Ever

My wife works with giving spiritual direction to younger women. From time to time, she will ask the women to write down one thing they have learned since they have entered adulthood. Or she might ask, "What would you tell yourself if you met yourself ten years ago?" Almost invariably, they will say something like this: "I would tell myself not to take things so seriously." Sometimes she will ask them to write down the one thing they were most worried about exactly one year ago. Often, they can't even remember. Their amnesia concerning old worries is an excellent springboard for asking whether their current anxieties are truly warranted.

Laughter helps us keep the right perspective, and some people and some cultures seem to cultivate this perspective naturally. For me, humor, and especially wit, doesn't come too naturally. So sometimes I clinch my teeth and try to learn humor. My church growing up didn't have a tradition of giving anything up for Lent in preparation for Easter. But, as an adult, sometimes I practice giving up something for the celebration of the Resurrection time. One year, I decided on the ambitious project of giving up seriousness.

My discipline for each of the 40 days of Lent was to learn one new joke a day. Hard to believe that someone would be so dogged about something so lighthearted, isn't it?

I wrote each joke down on a 3-by-5-inch card and filed it. They were terrible jokes. Sometimes I got the jokes out of old, used joke books. Here's an example of the kind of joke I learned: Did you hear about the dentist that married a manicurist? They fought tooth and nail. Organizer that I am, I still have those joke cards 25 years later. I could tell you a lot more of those kinds of jokes if you wanted me to.

The tooth and nail joke was one of the better jokes. The bottom line for me is that laughter does really seem to help when someone is imprisoned by some circumstance. We make the choice to laugh, especially if we can laugh at ourselves.

In the long view, one of the most remarkable things about Jesus is His confidence in who He is, combined with an amazing humility and the ability to not indulge in pomposity. Humor is hard to translate across cultures, and especially across thousands of years, but I think that Jesus is quite funny when He paints the picture of a poor man studiously trying to pull a speck out of his friend's eye when he has a huge log hanging out of his own eye. Every time he turns or tries to adjust for the light for his refined procedure, he whacks someone else with that plank (Matthew 7:1–5).

I saw a movie a long time ago where the scene with Jesus washing the disciples feet is played in a lighthearted way. The disciples clench their teeth and refuse to do the menial work. Jesus is smiling and gently poking fun at the disciples' "dignity." By washing their feet, Jesus doesn't have to say anything, and He gives them a chance to be involved in the fun in the future. At the very least, Jesus shows His own lack of that false self-importance, a self-importance that hits most of us. If you don't think you have it, watch your own emotions the next time you are in a group and someone is asked to volunteer to clean the toilets.

I guess we will never know in this life, but I think that Paul might have had to grow in the area of humor. He certainly had the praise thing down, singing to God after being beaten and imprisoned and all. He might have had a naturally fierce temper, chasing down Christians before his own conversion. Even later in life, we might see a hint of that ferocity. When Ananias has him struck in Jerusalem, he shoots right back, *"God is going to strike you, you whitewashed wall!"* (Acts 23:3). Soon thereafter he seems to recover and changes his tone.

We know he thought about some of the issues of the confinements of self-importance. He probably did some of his thinking about it when he was in jail. He seems to see the wonder of Christ, who empties himself, and doesn't think equality with God is something to be grasped (Philippians 2:1–10).

In 1 Corinthians 13, Paul writes some of the most practical things about love that I have ever read. At one point, he says that love does not insist on its own way. Paul goes even further. He says that love is not irritable or resentful. To be honest, irritability is my challenge right now. I think that in some ways, irritability is the lack of a sense of humor. I begin to think that my plans and my work are far more important than other people's plans. Anything that might hinder what I am doing is seen as a needless obstruction, and a cause for rightful irritation. Subconsciously, I am thinking that anyone who doesn't recognize my importance, my humility, my service, is a cause for me to be peevish or resentful. I can even work myself up to being self-righteous about my irritation. I have forgotten that being in a stew of irritability is a sin against love, perhaps much more of a sin against love than the act that is causing the irritability. Humor and laughter is an antidote to this kind of stinking thinking.

I heard someone quote the Christian philosopher Søren Kierkegaard and claimed that he said, "I want that humility that knows no humiliation." I haven't been able to track that quote down, but I think the essence of the idea can help us as we learn what being humble really is.

David learned a certain kind of humiliation. Perhaps humility became clearer to him during the years he was a fugitive and homeless. Later in his life, when he was bringing the Ark of the Covenant to Jerusalem, the Scripture says that he danced before the Lord. It must have been quite a dance. There seems to be questions about the appropriateness of his dress. It disgusted his wife, who watched him dance and leap before the Lord when she looked out the window. The Scripture says she despised him in her heart. Perhaps she remembered that she was the daughter of a king, and he was originally just a shepherd. Perhaps her own sense of importance was called into question.

We talked in an earlier chapter about the fact that we can choose whether to despise or not despise someone. It is a terrible but very common thing, when a person chooses to despise his or her spouse. When she makes her accusation to David, he refuses to allow his spirit to be dampened. He asserts that God chose him, and he will make merry before the Lord. David goes even further in a lack of false self-importance. *"I will make myself even more contemptible,"* he says, *"and I will be abased in your eyes." As often happens, the one who chooses to despise finds a worse situation afterwards* (2 Samuel 6:21–23).

Chaos Theory and a Mother's Hat

Self-respect is so important, and our generation has fought vociferously for self-respect. The prison of a sense of inferiority can be so confining. Yet the prison of a false self-importance can also be a horrible prison. You never know what seemingly small choices can result in. Chaos theory in the last 50 years has helped us think again about how very small modifications can make huge differences in the long term. We have famously talked about the wing of a butterfly eventually causing a whole series of complex results and changing the course of a hurricane on the other side of the world. We know this truth in the biblical world also, where some seemingly unimportant act can have huge implications down the road.

I remember particularly the story of a man who has been dead for many years now. He was homeless for a while. Once he was seriously stabbed in our neighborhood and almost died. He showed a great kindness to others and was well known in the local park. But he could surely get mad if anyone hurt his feelings or challenged his dignity. He could easily become resentful at a passing comment someone made. This tendency, which he took great pride in, had become a prison. It had forced him into difficult circumstances, where he found himself unemployed and cut off from his family.

He had become a Christian in later life, and God had begun to develop the natural kindness deep within him. Still, he struggled with his resentments, which could make him quit any endeavor in an instant, if he sensed some hint of insult.

He began to attend out mission church, and I remember his telling me a story about his mother long ago. "We never went to church when I was a kid," he said. "Mom told us that she went to church once, and some kids there laughed at her hat." At that moment, this man's chest swelled and his face took on a sense of pride in his mom. "She never went to church again," he said, as if her strong action somehow punished the church.

Now I know that when you don't want to do something, just about any excuse will do. Still, this story made me very sad. Who did her mother think she was punishing?

The kids at the church? They probably never gave it a second thought, and certainly didn't think about her. Did she think she was punishing the church at large? Or perhaps she thought she was punishing God. In reality, her action only punished herself.

And perhaps she unknowingly punished her own children. In the vein of chaos theory, I thought about what might have happened if she had taken a slightly different approach. What if she had laughed along with the kids, and showed them she realized that most hats adults wear are funny? What if she had forgotten the incident, and instead of fuming through the church service, she had genuinely listened to what God was doing there? What if she had shrugged her shoulders at how imperfect we all are, including the rude children and herself? What if she had kept going to the church and poured her life out in helping others through that same church?

And what if she had brought her children there, faithfully and diligently, refusing to allow her feelings to be hurt? The man I knew might have had a different script instilled in him, one of love instead of resentment. He might have found some more positive mentors than the ones he adopted as a teenager. He might have grown in faith and been able to love a woman responsibly, and marry, and have a job, and bless many others. He had all the qualities to do so, except for that resentment on any minor infringement of his own self-importance. He learned that lesson of resentment from his mother quite well.

I am grateful that God did a transforming work in him, and he did bless others before he died. I know that God never tells us what might have been. But I do know that thin-skinned self-importance can become its own sort of prison. It can be a confinement far more terrible than a prison with stone walls, if we forget to laugh.

principle #10
Become Dependent—The Prison of Fear

"I sought the Lord, and he answered me and delivered me from all my fears."

PSALM 34:4

"Worry is a cycle of inefficient thoughts whirling around a center of fear."

—*Corrie ten Boom*

Good Fear and Bad Fear

*I*t all depends on how you use the words. I suppose there is a good fear and a bad fear. Recently, I was at the North Rim of the Grand Canyon. We were walking along the edge of one of the trails. I was surprised (and indignant) that there wasn't more railing. The wind seemed to blow outrageously, and I thought I was going to be knocked over. I often pride myself in not being afraid of heights. I worked as a roofer part of the time to get through college. I could handle a 100-foot drop with no problem. I could work right on the edge. But this drop looked as though it were several thousand feet. I felt the adrenaline and the fear rise up in me. I tried to act tough, but I really just wanted to get off of that ledge. I suppose that emotion can be positive when a kind of fear keeps me from doing something needlessly dangerous. There is a type of awareness in some kinds of fear.

My dad would sometimes tell the story of the farmer who watched a bull charge a locomotive head-on. The farmer said of the bull, "I admire his courage. I don't think much of his judgment." Fear can give our foolish intentions a balance in a certain kind of judgment.

Then there is the fact that the Bible, especially older translations, uses the phrase, *"fear of God." "The fear of the Lord,"* Proverbs tells us, *"is the beginning of knowledge"* (1:7). Because of our current use of the word *fear*, some Bible translations will use a word *honor*, or *reverence*, or *awe* in these verses.

There is a truth in the fact that we honor, reverence God, that we don't take God for a fool, or take God for granted, in some "cheap grace" kind of way. In a sense, once we fear God, we will not fear what any humans do.

A kind of choice hangs over our lives in this respect. Dietrich Bonhoeffer, the German theologian who had to make some excruciatingly tough choices in his life, said that you have a choice—you can choose to fear God instead of the many things which you currently fear. The Bible talks a lot about fear, and the right kind of fear. When the people of God were looking at a political reality that seemed deadly unless they rushed to certain political alliances, God told Isaiah, *"Do not call conspiracy all that this people calls conspiracy, and do not fear what they fear, nor be in dread. But the Lord of hosts, him you shall honor as holy. Let him be your fear, and let him be your dread"* (8:12–13). In other words, once you regard God rightly, you won't be fearful of all these other circumstances, the things that other people are fearing.

So depending on how we use words, there may be a good fear, and there seems to be a bad fear. In terms of recovering and becoming free, I want to talk about that particular kind of fear, that crippling, paralyzing fear. This kind of fear keeps a person in the same place year after year. In my experience, if anything can be a prison, fear can be a prison. Fear keeps the person from ever moving forward. Like the cattle that never go near the wire because it once gave them an electric shock but no longer has a charge, we allow fears to keep us confined, even though the circumstances have changed. I hate this kind of fear.

This kind of fear is at the heart of our alienation from God. From the beginning, this fear has been a core result of our own sin. Eating of the fruit of the knowledge of good and evil is supposed to make Adam and Eve like God, but instead they hide from God when He comes. When God asks the deep question, *"Where are you?"* then Adam's answer is telling. *"I heard the sound of you in the garden, and I was afraid"* (Genesis 3:10). Here is the fear that the serpent has played upon—that God is in some ways selfish, that He is withholding good from Adam and Eve, that He does not have their best interests in His heart, that they must somehow find their own way without God to survive. When we sin we are lost forever. We know how familiar this script is today. This story is not what happened, but what happens.

In one way or another, if we are honest, we all have to face this sense of alienation and aloneness in this life at some time, in some way. In response, we will have to make a choice either to have faith or to have fear. Fear to me is the choice of unfaith, the confidence that the worst will happen and that God does not have our best interests at heart. Faith to me is living in the ultimate confidence that God will use all things for good for those who love him, regardless of how difficult the current circumstances seem.

In order to cope, fear may latch on to some crutch to get through some intellectual doctrine, some medication, some replacement to fill the void. Faith is the choice to trust God in spite of the circumstances, to believe that the worst thing is not the last thing.

The more I read the Bible, the more I think that this kind of fear, this faith that the worst will happen, is always forbidden. This kind of fear is never good. It doesn't have a use both ways. It isn't like anger. We are told to be slow to anger. But, sometimes our anger seems to be understood. Paul says be angry but do not sin (Ephesians 4:26). Except when speaking of that special reverence toward God, I don't see where the Bible says "Be fearful." In fact, we are sometimes reminded that the Bible says "fear not" 365 times or so. I haven't counted them, but I see these instructions all over the place.

Yet, let's be honest. It is so easy to say that we should not fear. Our battlegrounds are often quite different, so we can confidently be bold where someone else is fearful. However, we usually have some battleground of fear ourselves, if we take a moment to look at things. Fear often feels so much like a power beyond us. When you are having a panic attack, it is hard to hear someone say, "Be strong." It is not the right time. It is like giving swimming instructions to someone who is drowning.

Fear can seem like a democratic power, not preying on just one type of person. We can be gripped by the fear of what people say, or the fear of financial loss, or the fear of succeeding, or the fear of failure, or the fear of loneliness, or the fear of fear, or the fear of people, or the fear of sickness, or the fear of an insignificant life, or any toxic combination of these anxieties. In the end, the fears connect to God in the deepest sense. John Donne touches that deepest fear in his evocative lines from his honest poem,

> *"A Hymn to God the Father":*
> I have a sin of fear, that when I have spun
> My last thread, I shall perish on the shore.

Incidentally, Donne is another of those earlier poets who fought his own fears with a pun or two. He concludes his poem with the affirmation to God:

> "And, having done that, Thou hast done;
> I fear no more."
>
> — John Donne

"Thou hast done." "Donne" is pronounced like *done*.
—Get it?

Some people seek to hide this fear of ultimate abandonment. Perhaps these fears all connect to that fear of ultimate loss, a fear that eventually every relationship on earth, every position, every beauty in this life, will be lost. It is the fear that we will perish on the shore. This fear of ultimate loss, or a kind of death, can take a stranglehold on everything we do and every decision we make. This fear of ultimate separation is a prison.

The Book of Hebrews deals with this kind of slavery. Christ's activity is described as a freedom act from this kind of bondage:

> *"Since therefore the children share in flesh and blood, he himself likewise partook of the same things, that through death He might destroy the one who has the power of death, that is, the devil, and deliver all those who through fear of death were subject to lifelong slavery"* (2:14–15).

This passage cuts to the core of upside-down freedom. Instead of setting those in bondage free with some violent act, the liberator takes on the same kind of oppression those who are enslaved fear—a humiliating and agonizing death. Inversely, according to Hebrews, we are no longer subject to the fear of death, which is a kind of slavery that lasts a lifetime. Just as I see as I work with recovery, the Bible sees this kind of fear as a lifelong slavery.

The key to breaking out of this kind of fear is not, ironically, working to become more independent, to move to what social workers have sometimes called, "a more self-sustaining mode." The key is to do the opposite—to become more dependent. However, this new dependence is a particular kind of dependence.

This inverse revelation is what we continue to find as we work with people who are seeking to break free from the prison of constricting fear. In reality, when we focus exclusively on the circumstances, we are taking a self-defeating path. This is the way of worry, and no matter how self-righteously wise we think we are, when we meditate on the worst things that can happen, this exclusive focusing on the circumstances actually produces more fear.

However, when we choose to focus on God, we find another byproduct—courage. We don't have to manufacture it; it just happens. This is one of the reasons so many very important instructions begin to sound cliché. "Bring it to God," or "pray about it," or "be sure to have a quiet time." These phrases have become hackneyed because they have consistently been found to work.

The Best Time to Triangulate

When my wife counsels younger women concerning the fears they deal with, she often uses the image of a triangle. We are one point, the circumstances are another corner, and God is the third corner of the triangle. She says that no matter how often in human relationships, triangulating is a cop-out, here is one time that it is important to triangulate. If you only focus on you and the circumstances (one side of the triangle), fear and anxiety will result. But when you include God, no matter how difficult the issues are, wisdom and courage begin to emerge. As Alcoholics Anonymous often says in many other circumstances, "It works when you work it."

The key then, is not to become freely independent, at least not in this situation. The key is to develop the attitude of perpetual dependence, to choose to bring God into the circumstances. It is what Adam did not want to do when he hid. We continue to wonder what would have happened if Adam and Eve realized their rebellion, and ran to God in the garden, and accepted responsibility instead of working to shift the blame to someone else. George McDonald, the nineteenth-century Christian writer, used to say, "There is no escaping God but by running into His arms."

It is a truism that people often talk about what they don't have. You talk about money when you don't have much. People who are eminently wealthy are often silent about it.

You talk about grades if you are having some trouble there. People who have no trouble with making good grades are usually quiet when the subject comes up.

David must have had some issues with fear. He certainly had reason to fear. When we read the lyrics of his popular songs in Psalms, the subject of fear comes up often. David seems to engage in a kind of "self-talk." When David says, *"Yea though I walk through the valley of the shadow of death, I will fear no evil,"* he is not talking really for God's sake. He is including God in his life, but he seems to be talking to himself. It seems as though he finds that when he includes God, something happens. After he was homeless and had to pretend as though he were insane, he sings, *"I sought the Lord, and he answered me and delivered me from all my fears"* (Psalm 34:4). All his fears.

David must have had fear issues. He talks about fear so much. One of the psalms says, *"In the multitude of my anxieties within me, Your comforts delight my soul"* (94:19 NKJV). There were a multitude of fears. Yet from Goliath on, David seemed such a warrior, so courageous. It seems as though David continues to bring his circumstances to God, to include God, to triangulate. David, God, and his circumstances all become part of the triangle. It is a clear decision. *"When I am afraid, I put my trust in you,"* he sings, when the Philistines have seized him (56:3). Once again, we see David, that fugitive, that homeless person, choosing to put words of faith in his mouth, to make words of faith his script, rather than the words of fear.

"I have purposed that my mouth shall not transgress," he says. *"Concerning the works of men, by the word of Your lips I have kept away from the paths of the destroyer"* (17:3–4 NKJV). He sees that the destroyer can build a wall of false reality around the person through their own words, often words of fear. David supports a replacement policy—replacing words of fear with

words of faith. *"The Lord is on my side; I will not fear. What can man do to me?"* (Psalm 118:6 NKJV).

Not that he doesn't have fears, and doesn't acknowledge them. But again, his fears seem like a process, not an address. He doesn't allow himself to live in a world of constant fear, though his life is very dangerous, from the world's standpoint. In terms of personal bondage and personal freedom, Luther's words seem more and more practical as life proceeds. Thoughts of fear may come upon you, but you can decide how to deal with them. "You can't stop a bird from flying over your head, but you can keep him from building a nest in your hair," Luther is said to have stated concerning temptation.

The Real Heroes

Sometimes, under God's direction, you are going to have to do the thing you fear. Often we will find that part of our fear is mere unfamiliarity. Years ago, I had to deal with a fear that I was bringing my little children and wife into a neighborhood that had a reputation at the time (no more), of being crime-ridden. I had a fear for my little two-year-old and two-month-old. But my wife and I knew we needed to do it, so we did it. It is true that we lived next to a crack house and had to sweep the crack vials away from our front door. But we found that much of our fear was simply the fear of the unknown, as we found the closest relationships in any neighborhood that we have ever known.

I sometimes joke with parents in "crime-ridden" neighborhoods who will not let their kids go on a camping trip or outing in the country with our mission. They have read a headline or seen a movie where someone got killed in the country.

On the other hand, I have often talked to parents from the suburbs who used to have concerned looks on their faces as their son or daughter came for a while to our neighborhood. They had seen a violent television show and the buildings in our part of town were utilized as a backdrop. For both groups of parents, the ones in the city and in the suburbs, the unknown was a major part of the fear.

My wife went through a stage where she had an unreasonable fear of flying. As she prayed to God, she felt that she simply needed to walk into this fear and just do it, regardless of how she felt. As she simply flew over and over, eventually, the fear lifted. Once again, the missionary Hudson Taylor's axiom held true. Fears seem sometimes like an impossible wall. Taylor said, "First it is impossible, then it is difficult, then it is done." My wife looked back one day at her fear of flying, and saw that it had lifted. The fear was simply gone.

We cannot deny that the consequences of fear can be devastating. Fear can keep the slaves from the Promised Land. Fear can keep us from what God has for us. The people of God heard about the giants in the new land. The spies said that they felt like grasshoppers compared to these enemies. The people of God had already defeated themselves. They had a mind cage. It took the people of God a long time to work through it.

When we really begin to think about fear and courage, heroes begin to abound in our lives, no matter how dreary and routine our existence once seemed. I think about people in my life who have been liberated from fear. I think about people who have faced devastating fear, fear from mental illness, fear from abuse, fear from a damaging script instilled in them. Each of them decided to become "dependent," to turn to God, and through God, to face their fear in a brave way. I watch them quietly get up each day, help others, make the courageous choice of kindness when they have been trained most of their life to lash out in fear. I see people who make the courageous choice of patience in horrible circumstances, of choosing faith when others around them have already chosen despair. These others secretly mock the quiet people's stand for God. I watch these quiet people through service, in little unseen ways, take a stand every day, to be true freedom fighters, not just talking heads. They make all those around them more free, even when we don't realize what or who has caused the freedom. To these silent heroes over fear, to these freedom fighters over anxiety, I am unspeakably grateful. They inverted things. They took the mundane, unannounced back door toward freedom, and somehow came out standing in front.

conclusion
Remembering the Endgame

"That the creation itself will be set free from its bondage to decay and obtain the freedom of the glory of the children of God."

ROMANS 8:21 NSRV

"You Christians look after a document containing enough dynamite to blow all civilization to pieces, turn the world upside down. . . . But you treat it as though it is nothing more than a piece of literature."

—*Mahatma Gandhi*

His Mind Was a Bad Neighborhood

*H*e wouldn't look me in the face. He looked down at his big hands, hands that had made homemade tattoos up and down his arms while he was in prison. He was surly, and didn't have much to say. It was the visitation time at the prison. It had taken me a long time to get there, but I could hardly imagine what was going on in his mind during that time.

I remembered something another person had told me as I was trying to understand her actions. She simply said, "My mind is a bad neighborhood. You don't want to go there alone." I thought that this man may have felt the same way about his insides. They were a bad neighborhood. Who would want to visit *that* place?

I knew a little of his family background. He had grown up in the Lower East Side, and he had lived with his mother for a while in an abandoned building. I don't think he went to school much. His mother had a restraining order on the father, who had been brutal and abusive. Life in an abandoned building at that time and place could be brutal. You couldn't call the police if something went wrong. You were there illegally to begin with. Violence, or the threat of violence, seemed to keep things in line. Drugs were simply part of the diet. He himself, as he grew up, had tried to choke his mom to death. He had tried to physically intimidate me before, too, before he was locked up. It was tempting to just say that some people needed to be locked up. That was all they were good for.

"When I get out of here, I am going to be a rock star," he told me. He didn't know how to play a guitar. He was not musical. His looks were against him.

"Here is my newest tattoo," he mumbled, showing me some inked in numbers he had put on his bicep. He claimed he did it with a safety pin. He had a cut over his eye. I didn't ask him how he got it.

I felt a wave of fatigue and discouragement flow over me. What can Christ do for him? This man had so many strikes against him before he even started. Can I promise him that everything will be alright and that someday he will be a fulfilled, productive, successful part of our society? Can I give him some theological insights from my seminary training that will make him feel free? Can I give him a big smile and say that everything in his world is going to be just fine?

No. To be honest, this man may never be functional in a way that can be evaluated by a social worker, or even a missionary who is looking for a story to tell. But there is something I can tell him. I can still tell him about a God who will make a new earth and one day wipe every tear from his eye. One day God will make all things right. I can turn to the last page of the Bible and talk about the endgame (Revelation 21:1–5). I can tell him about the time when the drama of this life will be over, when the playwright walks out on stage and says that the play is done. I can tell him about a time when space and time as we know it will end, and how God, through Christ, will be revamping the whole show, and that this young, broken man somehow has a part to play in that new show. It's a show that very well may go beyond the bounds of time and space as our feeble minds know it now.

Whatever substantial healing and freedom we pray for in this life, we may never see total healing, or total freedom. At least not yet. But we both can know that God is making a place for us, a place where there is no disease, no poverty, no addiction, and yes, no bondage. According to the Bible, there is both safety and freedom, both appropriate boundaries and endless open doors in this new space. It is a place where the walls are high for security and the gates are always open. In this new kind of living place, *"its gates will never be shut by day — and there will be no night there"* (Revelation 21:25). Praise God. It isn't yet, but it is coming. We see samples of its inner freedom here, we see trickles of the waterfall of healing that is to come, but whatever we see now is only a hint of that openness, that liberation, that *"freedom of the glory of the children of God"* (Romans 8:21). According to this verse, *"creation itself will be set free."*

These promises are no opiate for the people. We learn every day that things work from the inside out. Once we really see on the inside where we are headed, things ironically begin to change in the present.

As we see that the now is not yet the endgame, that God is planning to do more than we can think or imagine, then we can begin to see the path to what seems unthinkable. Without this deep understanding of the liberating direction of all things, we are just sitting in the visiting rooms of the prisons, nodding our heads in superficial sympathy, with nothing more than some vague platitudes to share.

Once we see what God has done in Christ, then we can respond. Once we see that God wants us to be free, free in the largest sense of the word, to be a "free spirit," so to speak, then we can begin to trust and let go of what we thought was the steering wheel.

In the Gospel of John, Christ is the Bread and He gives the bread. He is the Light and He gives the light. He is the

Living Water and He gives the living water. He is the Word, and He gives the Word.

He tells us that if we remain in His Word, we are truly His disciples (John 8:31). Then we will know the truth, and the truth will set us free (8:32). Staying in the Word sometimes doesn't feel like the way to freedom.

We started this book with a true story of some firefighters who thought they knew the way to escape the fire. They were instructed to do the exact opposite by their foreman. They decided to disregard his instructions and make a run for freedom. Most of them perished. As we noted at the beginning, sometimes life is like that. We may have to do the opposite of what we first expected in order to be free.

An Upside-Down Review

*I*n review, the words of Jesus sometimes sound like the opposite of what we would expect. Losing our life in order to find it. Confining ourselves within His words in order to be free. But it really is quite simple. Once we dwell in His words, we begin to learn to truly hate the mind cages, the evil that entraps us. Once we dwell in His words, we can even limit our expression instead of expanding it, in order to refrain from a constant pattern of blaming others. Instead of broadening our destructive emotions, we can learn to narrow our focus. Then we can turn from the roiling family anger and make a free choice to rejoice in the right.

Oddly enough, when we do these things, even in spite of ourselves, our attitude begins to change. We can see stone walls as opportunities instead of bondage. We even learn to build walls in the right place instead of the wrong place, to set boundaries and limitations that ironically lead to freedom.

We are led to insight about our own world, and we move to stop chasing the banality of the values of the world around us. We can limit our activities instead of increasing them and inversely do more. We learn to look beyond the choking prison of ourselves, and begin to give when it seems we have nothing. As the road to freedom gets brighter, we learn to refuse the perpetual opportunities to get discouraged and face those opportunities with the right kind of stubbornness.

Instead of working to protect our dignity, we can even start to laugh at our own seriousness. In the end, we break that bondage of fear, the prison that keeps us from life. Inversely, by becoming more dependent on God, we find a different kind of independence than the kind that is always trying to manufacture some shred of courage.

That's why Jesus says that as we continue in His Word, we will know the truth and the truth will set us free (John 8:32). Then, Jesus says, we will stop having these false ideas of a limited freedom. Things are turned upside down, and we are no longer a *"slave of sin"* (John 8:34). We get a glimpse of real freedom, beyond the pale of our limited circumstances. We get a glimpse of real freedom through what Christ has done. *"So if the Son sets you free, you will be free indeed"* (John 8:36). Finally. Freedom didn't come the way we thought it would.

At first, it doesn't seem easy to face these challenges. Quite the opposite. The challenges usually, at first, seem overwhelming. But as we respond to the bigness of what God has done in Christ, we find that the words we have repeated from Hudson Taylor become more and more true. First it is impossible. Then it is difficult. Then one day, surprisingly, it is done. That is often how freedom in any sphere works, whether it is freedom from heroin or freedom from constant, petty worry.

So what can I say to this young man in prison, who seems to have so much against him? He is in jail. His mind seems like a cage. His patterns are self-destructive.

When I was a young man, I worked in a community service location in Harlem. I was going to seminary, and my mind was twisting and turning during the week through many seemingly important theological and intellectual conundrums. It was a well-endowed and wealthy seminary, and it was easy to talk about what should be in such a lovely, manicured place.

On the weekends, I would go to Harlem to work. This was the 1970s in New York City, when a bankrupt city seemed unable to provide the basic services for its people in many neighborhoods. In the area where I worked, there were many abandoned buildings, and drugs and anger ran together down the streets. I became angry too. On hot summer days, I didn't think that I had much that was practical to offer in this situation. I thought about leaving seminary and going to law school. That approach seemed much more serviceable to people who were being arrested and incarcerated.

One day, as I was fuming about what choice to make, I realized something. A lawyer can help a person get free from jail, but a representative of God's grace can help people become free, no matter where they are. A lawyer can help lift the physical burden of someone who is oppressed, but a minister of the great news can help a person be free regardless of circumstances. Free indeed.

The Largeness of It

So what can I bring to this young man with his homemade tattoos in prison? I can bring something more than some legal papers, more than intellectual advice. I can start with the bigness of God's presence and His plan. The largeness of it.

It is so big, we can hardly speak of it. It is so big, we forget about it in our petty bustling through our church work. His desire to set us free is stronger than our desire to be free. When we begin to see it, we will say, "of course." The good news of God is in every book of the Bible, in my view, but I love especially the way that Paul shares it in Ephesians. Once more, as Paul writes this book, he is in prison. Naturally. In chapter 1, he says that God is making known the secret of his will, which he set forth in Christ, *"as a plan for the fullness of time"* (v. 10). This is the build-up part of the sentence.

Then comes the rest of the sentence with the plan: "To unite all things in him, things in heaven and things on earth" (v. 10). This plan is so big, everything is covered—things in heaven and things on earth. It is bigger than I can conceive of. It bursts the bounds of my expectations. The poet Alfred Tennyson once said, "Our little systems have their day; They have their day and cease to be: They are but broken lights of thee, And thou O Lord art more than they."

In Ephesians, the punch line is this: To unite all things in Christ. Beyond any little system I might think of, God is planning to unite all things in the goodness and sacrificial love of Christ. All things will be mended, made whole, and brought together. He says that it will happen in heaven and on earth, in every system and time that we can imagine, through every planet, every galaxy, through every dimension that Paul or any contemporary theoretical physicist can possibly conceive of. According to the Bible, the plan is that large, and even larger.

Paul, the imprisoned one, confined by chains and walls, is unafraid to use big language. What God is doing is bigger than prisons, bigger than addictions, bigger than our discouragement, bigger than all the barriers and destructive scripts that grip our lives.

At another time, Paul writes his letter to the Romans. He isn't in prison, but he is still thinking about bondage. He talks not only about the fact that we will be set free in Christ, but that creation itself will be set free. *Creation* is a big word. Think of it. Hundreds of millions of stars and galaxies and we don't know what else, maybe hundreds and millions of universes, all will be set free. Everything created, books and planets and swans and cell phones and giraffes and sewage systems, whatever that is in our realm of cognition and all that is not will be set free. These words are worth repeating. Paul says that creation itself will *"obtain the freedom of the glory of the children of God"* (8:21). Wow. This is the endgame that we often forget.

So what would I bring to that poor man in prison, a man with few cards to play in life and little hope? God's big plan. I mean big plan. Not limited in time or space or this life.

I mentioned earlier my close friend who said that in 1 trillion years, none of these truths will really matter. A trillion years is simply beyond my ability to understand. The life of animals, people, stars, and galaxies pale in the light of 1 trillion years. Languages, civilizations, life itself seem miniscule in light of these vast measures. Paul says tongues and knowledge itself will one day pass away (1 Corinthians 13:8). If language and knowledge itself became something different than what we could conceive of, what would still be true?

My answer was that one reality still would matter, regardless of the shape of universes to come. That reality is the sacrificial love that Christ showed. That truth, regardless of the way or language or means it is communicated, is the core of existence. It always will be.

That sacrificial love of God through Christ is the big plan I bring to the one who is in prison. Plus God shows a way. What I have learned is that the same inverted principles we have talked about in this book apply when someone is physically in jail, or physically addicted. In fact, the same upside-down principles apply in any kind of bondage. Bondage can grip the insecure man who works on Wall Street to acquire more and more wealth, or the unsure woman seeking validation in all the wrong places and in all the wrong relationships, or the chronically unhappy, or the consistently selfish, people uneasily unaware that their mind is gripped by a cage that they cannot see.

Things Just Don't Go as Planned

et's be honest. Things don't turn out the way we think they should so many times. We see it in our own lives. We certainly see it in the lives of the characters in the Bible. Moses comes back to help set free his people and lead them to the Promised Land. But in the end, he doesn't get there himself. David is anointed early as king, but then finds himself a homeless fugitive for years. Later, even though he is a man after God's own heart, his personal failures jeopardize his family and he finds himself as an older man betrayed by his own son. Paul wants to be the best of Pharisees, but is transformed by Christ instead, and finds himself in the humiliating position of staying in jail and ultimately being beheaded by the very Roman authorities through whom he had sought protection as a citizen. We don't even know if he ever got to Spain as he had hoped.

For me, all of their experiences are more spokes to the hub of Christ's journey. Christ shows us one underlying principle, that the worst thing is not the last thing. His own crucifixion was the worst thing.

I think that with my young friend in prison, I can point to that hub, that act of Christ which took the worst thing and used it to bring freedom for us. Christ is always turning people's expectations upside down. His whole life is upsetting to our conventional truths. Somehow, horrible things, even unspeakably unfair things, become a part of this new kind of power. Paul calls it *"resurrection power"* (Philippians 3:10). Mockery was a part of that resurrection power. Crucifixion, courts, beatings, and uncertainty were a part of that power, because there was something beyond those things. It seems as though anything can be a part of that power, if we look far enough ahead, and in the right direction.

This kind of power inverts our expectations on freedom. This kind of power is the kind at work when Jesus tells the religious people, so confident in their freedom as opposed to others, that the prostitutes and sleazy tax collectors will precede them to heaven. Huh? This kind of power gives hope, in the long view, to my sad friend in prison. He may find, in ways that would shock me to the core of my conventional being, that the very prayers that seem at first least answered, are finally, in the long run, beyond the galaxies, the ones most granted. Life has never been what we thought it was. It has always been a bit more upside down than we were prepared to admit.

The Bible ends with another writer who is once again in jail. Big surprise. His name is John. At the end of his book, which is the last book in our Bible, he speaks to his Lord along with the motley, harassed people of God. He says, *"Come, Lord Jesus!"* (Revelation 22:20). In looking at this prayer in prison, pointing toward the future hope, things still look a bit upside down. One Christian theologian put it this way: this prayer of hope "places the true starting point at the end." We should have expected that.

appendix
Gallery of the Uncarcerated

Incarcerated comes from the Latin word carcer, which means "prison." I am seeking to describe people, who have somehow turned prisons, sometimes literal prisons, inside out. They have inverted bondage and found freedom in the worst of situations. In order to describe these upside-down people, I have coined a new word: the uncarcerated. *Forgive me.*

Note: I did not list every single person cited in this book in the "Gallery of the Uncarcerated." I only listed those who I felt had particular insights to offer in further reading. Some of the people listed below are people with very different views than my own. A few would not claim to be Christian. However, each of them made a connection with something in the book. If I didn't include someone about whom I wrote, I often listed the source of information within the book itself.

Boethius—I think this sixth-century Christian philosopher should be read more. His *Consolation of Philosophy* was important in the Middle Ages. Sure, the book is a bit dense, but Boethius starts out pretty cranky about his imprisonment, and it is something to watch him progress. In the end, he refuses to let jail define him. We talk about him in principle #4, when we talk about the prison of attitude.

Niels Bohr—In one very specific sense, I think that Niels Bohr, the twentieth-century quantum physicist, and Martin Luther, the sixteenth-century biblical scholar, are kindred spirits. They both feel that some true things are paradoxical. Bohr thought that the opposite of a profound truth was another profound truth. I mention him in the introduction because I think his approach helps us think about freedom in a different way. Another quote of his I found online is this: "How wonderful that we have met with a paradox. Now we have some hope of making progress."

G. K. Chesterton—This English writer of the first part of the last century was one of the influences on C. S. Lewis. I think that his book *The Ball and the Cross* is underrated. The first time I read it, I thought it was a choppy patchwork of a wacky story. The second time I read it, I thought it was brilliant. For me, Father Michael is the key. We talk about Father Michael's achievement in principle #4.

Winston Churchill—I have included Churchill in the list because of the amazing persistence he showed. He had many serious opportunities to be deeply discouraged in his life, and sometimes he was. Somehow he found a way to get through and to help others do so. I like the fact that almost all the quotes we use from Churchill come from speeches he made after he was 65. He really didn't give in. We talk about it in principle #8. His speech at Harrow School is a gem, even without the famous quotes from it.

David—We quote David all through the book. He is a compelling, uncarceratedfigurebecausehewasontherunforalongtime.Thepeople I work with are sometimes homeless, and they appreciate that he lived in a cave. Some here see that as the equivalent of sleeping under a bridge. Yet his song lyrics give us a lot of insight into his journey to freedom. He must have been afraid a lot, but he rewrites his script in his songs and guards his words in order to move toward freedom. Even though he was anointed as a king, for a long time he was treated as a criminal. In our mission, we found his advice very practical.

Dorothy Day—This twentieth-century activist and radical Catholic lived in my area in New York City. You can still experience her influence. She writes movingly of making the choice to delight in routines of service that could seem brain-numbing and monotonous. We talk about this choice in principle #4. Her autobiography, *The Long Loneliness*, is a classic.

Francis of Assisi—I mentioned him in the introduction because some stories about him imply that he had to go through staying in a cave in order to understand the joy and freedom God had for him—a strange road to freedom. When I worked with Franciscans, they had an English omnibus of the writings about him. It had 1,960 pages and was a bit overwhelming.

Abraham Joshua Heschel—He was a twentieth-century rabbi who lost two sisters in concentration camps, and another sister and his mother to Nazi actions. I have mentioned Heschel in the introduction of this work because of the wonderful book he wrote about *The Prophets*. He refuses to take a superficial route as the prophets speak of God purpose, and freedom. The first half of the book was better than the second half, for the things I was interested in.

Richard Lovelace—Clearly a charming, dashing, attractive man, this seventeenth-century poet turns the tables on his imprisonment in "To Althea, from Prison." It is amazing how a little poetry, a little art, can redefine a situation. We talk about this reshaping in principle #4.

Norman Maclean—I have included Maclean among the gallery because of his fascination with how young men respond in the face of an enclosing fire in *Young Men and Fire*. He reflects in a profound way about why people do what they do in times of great need. I started my introduction, partially based on his account of the Mann Gulch Fire. I think it is a great book. He is better known for his other book, *A River Runs Through It and Other Stories* because of the movie that was taken from it.

Nelson Mandela—I think everyone should read Mandela's book *Long Road to Freedom*. With the kind of oppression and imprisonment he endured, he could have taken another road of revenge when he came to power. In principle #7, I talked about the way he uses his gardening in prison for others, even the wardens, as a parable for the new world he would be given responsibility in.

Jurgen Moltmann—This contemporary German theologian may be a strange one to cite in a book like this. However, I end the conclusion of this book with his comment on the end of the Bible—that the end is really the starting point. In *The Crucified God*, Moltmann reflected a great deal on the strangeness of God in Christ being abandoned on the cross, rejected by the inhuman persons as he identifies with the dehumanized. Because Christ's love extends to both the oppressors and the victims, a different kind of freedom emerges. Moltmann had been a German prisoner of war in World War II. He felt almost overwhelming remorse for what Germans had done after the war. He was given a pocket New Testament by an American chaplain. He said, "I didn't find Christ, He found me."

Moses—Moses in the Bible followed God's instructions to tell the people to give even though they were accustomed to very little. They were told to give up a lamb and Passover even when they had so little. They also gave up their wealth for the tabernacle. We speak of Moses and the people in principle #7 because they gave when they had nothing.

Paul of Tarsus—Paul is the biblical poster child for the "uncarcerated." He seems to have been in every jail in the Mediterranean, yet he doesn't seem caged. He rejoices when others would sulk, he sees chains as an opportunity, he sees his relationship with Christ as so much better than his former privileges. I wonder if the prisoners and guards associated with him thought he was nuts. Apparently, some of those co-prisoners and guards didn't think he was nuts in the end (Philippians 1:12–13).

Sir Walter Raleigh—I talk about Raleigh, the seventeenth-century adventurer and poet, in the chapter on not taking yourself too seriously (principle #9). He has a bunch of other humorous lines as he faces his own death. To a friend who said he would attend Raleigh's execution, he said, "I do not know what you may do for a place. For my part, I am sure of one; you must make what shift you can." He was big on puns. When he saw the axe that would behead him, he called it a "sharp medicine" and "a sure cure for all diseases." You might find the lines funnier if you were an Elizabethan living at the time.

Aleksandr Solzhenitsyn—I talk about this great Russian writer in chapter 6, as we resist the endless flow of busy and trivial information that barrages us. He was another incarcerated one, spending about 11 years in some kind of internment in the Soviet Union after World War II. His thought deepened, and he came to take a philosophic, Christian approach to the world. His insights in prison on freedom are profound. I can't resist including a longer quote from *The Gulag Archipelago* that helped me tremendously as I thought about life as a young man:

> "Do not pursue what is illusory—property and position: all that is gained at the expense of your nerves decade after decade, and is confiscated in one fell night. Live with a steady superiority over life—don't be afraid of misfortune, and do not yearn after happiness; it is, after all, the same: the bitter doesn't last forever, and the sweet never fills the cup to overflowing. It is enough if you don't freeze in the cold and if thirst and hunger don't claw at your insides. If your back isn't broken, if your feet can walk, if both arms can bend, if both eyes see, and if both ears hear, then whom should you envy? And why? Our envy of others devours us most of all. Rub your eyes and purify your heart—and prize above all else in the world those who love you and wish you well."

Hudson Taylor—He didn't seem to have remarkable qualities as a young man, but in principle #8, I mention this missionary's understanding of keeping with God's work, even when things look impossible. I continue to quote his insight on persistence to the end of the book. He spent 51 years in China.

Mother Teresa—With all her remarkable traits, it is her persistence that touches me. This woman, who started so small and shy, turned the world's understanding of freedom upside down. *Something Beautiful for God*, by Malcolm Muggeridge, is one good book about her. I mention her in principle #8.

George Washington—He refused to give up. His soldiers often didn't have provisions and pay. They grumbled. I refer to him in discussing the freedom to refuse to get discouraged in principle #8. *Almost a Miracle* by John Ferling is a good book about him.

*G*raffiti *C*ommunity *M*inistry

started in a storefront more than 35 years ago. Now it works to express God's love in tangible ways for thousands each year. It has also started Graffiti 2 in the South Bronx, Graffiti 3 in Brooklyn, and Gotta Serve in Long Island, as well as fostering and supporting over 20 new churches while acting as mother church, aunt church, or grandmother church. It partners with a number of other ministries in New York City in a commitment to do the small thing to serve the unserved. For more information, contact Graffiti Community Ministry at 205 E. 7th Street, New York, NY 10009, (212) 473-0044, or go to graffitichurch.org.

New Hope® Publishers is a division of WMU®, an international organization that challenges Christian believers to understand and be radically involved in God's mission. For more information about WMU, go to wmu.com. More information about New Hope books may be found at NewHopeDigital.com. New Hope books may be purchased at your local bookstore.

Use the QR reader on your
smartphone to visit us online at
NewHopeDigital.com

If you've been blessed by this book, we would like to hear your story.
The publisher and author welcome your comments and
suggestions at: newhopereader@wmu.org.

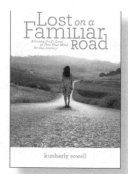